Teaching Gramn Punctuation and Spelling Through Drama

Visual, Auditory and Kinaesthetic Activities

Debbie Chalmers

Brilliant
PUBLICATIONS

Brilliant Publications publishes many other practical resource books for primary school teachers, a few of which are listed below. You may find more details on our website: www.brilliantpublications.co.uk.

Brilliant Activities for Reading Comprehension Series

Other publications

Published by Brilliant Publications
Unit 10
Sparrow Hall Farm
Edlesborough
Dunstable
Bedfordshire
LU6 2ES, UK

Tel: 01525 222292

E-mail: info@brilliantpublications.co.uk

Website: www.brilliantpublications.co.uk

The name Brilliant Publications and the logo are registered trademarks.

Written by Debbie Chalmers

Illustrated by Chantal Kees

Cover illustration by Kirsty Wilson

Front cover designed by Brilliant Publications

© Text: Debbie Chalmers 2013

© Design: Brilliant Publications 2013

ISBN: 978-1-78317-022-7

e-book ISBN: 978-1-78317-025-8

First printed and published in the UK in 2013

The right of Debbie Chalmers to be identified as the author of this work has been asserted by herself in accordance with the Copyright, Designs and Patents Act 1988.

Contents

Grammar Activities

Punctuation Activities

Spelling Activities

Introduction

Confident understanding and use of the English language, in speaking and listening, reading and writing, is important for success and achievement. Vital skills in basic literacy, including spelling, punctuation and grammar, must be developed and reinforced by teachers working with pupils in Key Stage 2, so that they can move from primary to secondary education with the ability to express themselves clearly and accept new challenges in all subjects and areas of learning.

Learning literacy through drama

Literacy skills are relevant to every interaction in a person's life and need not only be learned at a desk, but may be explored and developed through drama. Dramatic activities are visual, auditory and kinaesthetic and suit all types of learner. Too often, the more practical methods of teaching are reserved for those pupils who need extra support, or are hard to engage or challenging to work with, but, just because a pupil is able to learn skills from a book, that doesn't mean that it is the best or only way for him to learn. Opportunities to experience literacy and absorb ideas, skills and understanding through speech, movement and social interactions benefit all pupils and encourage them to feel, understand and remember on a deeper level, so that they may retain and draw on their stored knowledge whenever they need it in the future.

In groups and as individuals

Teachers' knowledge and understanding of individual pupils, and of their levels of ability and preferred learning methods, will enable them to use the activities in this book appropriately to offer useful and productive learning experiences for them all. Pupils may access the activities in their own ways and at their own levels, allowing a whole class to learn together despite a wide range of abilities. Mixed year group classes may particularly benefit from this approach. Smaller groups may also be taught separately to allow greater reinforcement of certain skills or more stimulation and challenge for particular pupils as appropriate.

Through games and activities

Pupils will learn more and retain their knowledge and understanding more easily if they are encouraged to use their imaginations to develop concepts and ideas in their own ways and to make activities relevant to themselves, their lives and their interests. The clearly explained ideas and suggested extensions in this book will provide inspiration and save time for busy teachers. The games and activities offer enough opportunities for healthy competition between individuals and groups and for pupils to challenge themselves, but emphasize working together so that everybody may learn, making the learning of literacy through drama constructive – and fun – for all pupils.

Preparing for learning

It is ideal to have access to a hall or another large clear room for most of the activities, but it is also possible to work in a classroom or smaller group area, simply by moving furniture back and rearranging the space. When the weather is good enough, many of the games may also be played outside in a playground or garden.

Many of the activities suggest making letters, words or parts of words on cards. Any type of card or paper may be used and, when necessary, the words may be attached to a wall with sticky tape, pins or Blu-tack. Stickers are sometimes suggested, but paper and sticky tape could be substituted if preferred. Teachers may choose to type and print their words, photocopy them, laminate them or provide them in a variety of colours, but, unless there is time and money to spare, there is no real need to do more than write clearly with a black marker pen. The quality and enthusiasm of the teaching is much more important to the pupils' learning than the quality of the props.

Often, it is valuable to involve the pupils in an activity right from the beginning, by inviting them to help to make the letters and words that they need. A well-organized, busy classroom can create more resources more quickly than a teacher sitting alone. It also produces more interested pupils, who are motivated to learn and absorb the concepts being explored.

Some of the activities require some preparation using resources readily available in a school, such as story and poetry books or dictionaries. Devoting a literacy session to these in the classroom during the preceding day or week will enable pupils to fully understand and develop the drama activity. Other games need no preparation at all and can be used when time is short or to provide a stimulating break for pupils between more sedentary activities. As a teacher uses this book and becomes familiar with it, he or she will be easily able to select appropriate and useful activities for different times.

Teachers may find it useful to keep a notebook in which they jot down any concepts that their classes are struggling to remember and any words that they particularly want to include in their pupils' learning. They may then use this information when choosing activities or planning lists of words to make.

It will be obvious that some of the activities are grouped together to explore, develop and extend one general topic, such as different types of word endings, or commas, or plurals. However, all of the activities are self-contained and may be used in any order and any number of times, with groups of any size or ability.

Developing and retaining knowledge

It is through regular exposure to words – looking at them, handling them, searching for them, moving them around, putting them together, pulling them apart, saying them aloud, discussing them, problem solving with them, miming and acting them, guessing them, changing them and playing games with them – that pupils will learn to read and write them, understand and remember them and use them confidently. Within a stimulating but relaxed environment containing drama, chatting and laughter, they will develop a rich vocabulary and a love of words that makes using language a pleasure.

Is that your name?

Learning objective

Proper nouns and common nouns

Preparation

Talk with your pupils about nouns, which are always naming words. Invite them to help you to find examples in books of proper and common nouns and to tell them apart by looking at whether the initial letter is capitalized or not. Then discuss which are written as proper nouns (names of people, places, days and months and also titles) and which are common nouns (names of animals, things, shapes, weather and seasons).

Activity

Ask the pupils to stand up and stretch their arms high above their heads to pretend to be proper nouns with capital letters, then to crouch down low to pretend to be common nouns written only with small letters. Invite them to practise by calling out their own names and standing up, then calling out *boy* and *girl* and crouching down.

Call out proper nouns and common nouns in a random order, for the pupils to respond to with their bodies. For example: *girl, October, dog, boy, England, triangle, Mr Smith, house, chair, table, Mrs Brown, Monday, tree, playground, Jungle Book, snow, Black Beauty, horse, winter.*

As the pupils grow more confident, include collective nouns, such as: *class, team, flock* or *pile,* and abstract nouns, such as: *happiness, misery, excitement* and *worry.*

Gradually increase the pace of the game too, until all of the pupils stretch or crouch quickly and no longer copy each other.

Extension/challenge

Suggest to the pupils that, often, common nouns are more general, while proper nouns are more specific. However, the addition of the article *the* can make a common noun more specific, as *'the tall house'* or *'the soft banana'* refers to a particular home or fruit, whereas *'a tall house'* or *'a soft banana'* could mean any home or fruit anywhere that happens to fit the description.

Divide the pupils into two equal groups and ask them to form two lines, facing each other. (If the group is large or space is limited, the lines could be semi-circular.) Both lines should start crouching down. The first child in one line stays crouching down and calls out a common name for a place, such as *town.* The first child in the second line, who is facing him, responds by giving a proper name for a specific place of that type, such as *Dunstable,* jumping up at the same time to indicate it needs a capital letter. Continue down the lines in this way. You may need to give some examples to help them to begin, such as:

> *beach – Blackpool*
> *forest – Thetford*
> *airport – Heathrow*

Repeat the game, putting together seasons and appropriate months, such as:

> *autumn – October*
> *summer – July*

Move on to people's names when the pupils are more confident. The more amusing the names, the better! Encourage ideas such as:

> *boy – Herbert*
> *girl – Trixiebell*
> *man – Mr Nobody*
> *lady – Mrs Woman*
> *farmer – Iona Pigg!*

Tell me more

Learning objective
Adjectives that describe nouns

Preparation
Make cards to represent simple nouns and an equal number of cards to represent different adjectives. Explain to your pupils that adjectives describe nouns, so they are placed beside names to answer the questions: What is it like? Can you tell me more about it?

Activity
Give one word card to each pupil and ask them all to walk around the room. The adjectives say their words over and over again quietly (eg *'blue, blue, blue'* or *'small, small, small'*) while the nouns mime their words (eg, playing a guitar or putting on a hat). Invite pupils to watch and listen in order to find a suitable partner and then to stand still together as a pair. For example:

brown	and	*cow*
tall	and	*tower*
new	and	*car*

Each pair may then demonstrate their description to the rest of the group in turn. If any pupil is unable to find a suitable partner, ask him to choose a noun or an adjective from a pair that has already performed and invite that person to take a second turn.

Extension/challenge
Suggest various themes and ask each pupil to think of a different related adjective for each one. Invite pupils to point to or mime their adjectives, in turn, for everybody else to guess. Begin with something simple, such as colours (to point to) or feelings (shown through facial expressions), and move on to more complicated ideas, such as shapes or textures. For example: *happy, sad, cross, tired, surprised, thinking* or *rough, smooth, soft, prickly, slippery, shiny.*

Teaching Grammar, Punctuation and Spelling Through Drama
© Debbie Chalmers and Brilliant Publications

Which one?

Learning objective
Adjectives of order

Preparation
Make a set of cards with number words on them – one for each pupil in the group. This may be 1 – 10, 1 – 19, 1 – 26, etc, depending on the size of your group.

Activity
Give one number card to each pupil and ask them to arrange themselves in a line in numerical order, to count from one, from left to right. Stand to the left of the line yourself and invite them to call out their numbers in order (*one, two, three,* etc), taking their cue from the pupil beside them. Call out *Zero!* yourself to begin.

Ask pupils to repeat the activity, calling out ordinal numbers instead: *first, second, third* and on up to *thirtieth* or beyond. Explain that these are a type of adjective because they can describe and distinguish between nouns and make them more specific. For example: *her third son* or *the twenty-first book*.

Ask pupils to hide their numbers and then to form groups of three randomly. Invite them to see how quickly they can show their numbers to each other, stand in order (1, 6, 18 or 7, 15, 22, etc) and call out in turn: *First! Middle! Last!* They should see that words such as *first, last, middle* and *in-between* can also work as adjectives. Think up some examples of this together, such as: *the first horse, the last jelly, the middle cushion* or *the house in-between*.

Extension/challenge
Invite pupils to help you to think of as many adjectives of size as possible, then to stand in a line (or more than one line if you have 30 children and only ten words), to order them. For example: *microscopic, minute, tiny, little, small, medium, large, big, huge, giant, enormous, gigantic*.

Ask the pupils to use their bodies to try to become the graded sizes, each a little bigger or taller than the previous one, beginning with a pupil curled up on the floor and ending with a pupil standing on tiptoe with arms outstretched.

As clever as that

Learning objective
Nouns and adjectives in similes

Preparation
Talk with your pupils about similes and well-known sayings. Find out which ones they already know and ensure that they are all aware that similes use the format: *'as'* (adjective) *as a* (noun)'. Make a list for your own use. For example:

> *as flat as a pancake*
> *as blind as a bat*
> *as fit as a fiddle*
> *as quiet as a mouse*
> *as thin as a rake*

Activity
Pupils can play this game as individuals or, if the class is large, you may prefer to give each word to a pair or a group of three who will mime it together. Secretly tell half of the pupils one noun each and the other half of the pupils one adjective each. (Make sure you choose words that will match to create similes!)

Invite the first group to mime their nouns (simultaneously), while the second group sit down to watch them and try to guess and remember what they all are. Then ask the two groups to swap roles.

Finally, ask all of the pupils to stand up and move around together and to find their partners to create correct similes, using only their memories. Pupils should check, by telling each other their words, when they think they have found each other and sit down together if they are correct. If any pupils cannot find a partner, suggest that they perform their mimes again as clues.

Extension/challenge
Invite pupils to form small groups (of three to six members) and to think up new similes of their own. Support them by offering more unusual ideas, such as:

> *as cuddly as a teddy*   or
> *as wet as a bucket of water*

Suggest to more able pupils that they could create exaggerations and contradictions, such as:

> *as useful as a chocolate radiator!*   or
> *as loud as a whispering grasshopper!*

These will be useful to remember in the future, when they want to add humour to their creative writing and poetry.

Encourage as much creativity and imagination as possible and enjoy making some fun similes together!

To do it together

Learning objective

Verbs – root forms

Preparation

Explain to your pupils that verbs are 'doing words' and that, in English, the root form of every verb is 'to –'. Make a list of verbs together (and photocopy it for extension activities). For example: *to smile*, *to clap*, *to sleep*, *to run*, etc.

Activity

Ask the pupils to sit in a circle and invite one to begin the game by miming a verb of his choice, such as *to dance*. The next pupil to the right may guess and name the verb and then the two can perform the mime together, ending it by saying the verb aloud: *To dance!* Continue the game by inviting the second pupil to mime another verb for the third to guess and then asking those two to perform and say the new verb together, such as: *To stamp!*

Repeat the activity around the circle, with each pupil taking his cue to perform and speak in turn, until the last pupil performs a mime for the first one to guess. (If your group is large, you may choose to have more than one circle playing the game simultaneously.)

Extension/challenge

Divide the pupils into two equal groups. Give a copy of the verbs list to each group and ask the pupils to choose one verb each.

Invite the two groups to walk towards each other, all miming their verbs, and challenge each pupil to find his 'partner', who is performing the same verb. Remind them that two people may interpret a word differently and the mimes may not look the same. As each two pupils find each other, they should stop and stand together to shout out their verb. For example: *To hop!*

© Debbie Chalmers and Brilliant Publications

Now or later?

Learning objective
Verb tenses

Preparation
Encourage your pupils to think of as many different verbs as possible and to create an action to match each one. For example: *to stamp, to crawl, to jump, to spin, to listen, to search, to freeze.*

Activity
Invite pupils to form groups of three and suggest one verb to each group. Ask the groups to mime the three tenses of their verbs, with one group member taking on each role. For example: *I stamped, I am stamping and I will stamp.*

The first pupil should complete the action and stop, to indicate the past tense, the second pupil should perform the action continuously, to indicate the present tense, and the third pupil should think about the action before beginning it, to indicate the future tense. (A mimed 'think' usually involves gazing into the distance while tapping a finger on the chin.)

Encourage pupils to discuss and negotiate to decide on their roles and to help each other to create the mimes. Invite each group to perform their actions in turn, for everybody else to watch.

Extension/challenge
Divide the pupils into three separate groups to represent the past, the present and the future tense. Ask them all to remember which group they are in and then to move around each other and sit down in spaces. Challenge the pupils to maintain concentration and take each cue correctly, jumping up when their tense is called and remaining seated when the others are called. Practise first, by calling out just the words past tense, present tense and future tense several times each in a random order, until all pupils understand the game.

Now ask pupils to listen carefully and to jump up and perform an appropriate action each time they hear a verb spoken in their tense. When you call out a verb in the past tense, a third of the pupils should jump up, complete their actions and then stop and sit down again. When you use the present tense, another third of the pupils should jump up and perform their actions continuously, until you call out a verb in the future tense, when they should sit down, to be replaced by the last third, who mime thinking and then beginning their actions.

Call out a variety of verbs, using the three tenses several times each in a random order and in different forms. For example:

Past tense
I hopped
I did jump
I have skipped
I was running

Present tense
I sing
I am whistling

Future tense
I will sleep
I am going to roll
I shall wriggle

Go on until the pupils can no longer keep up and praise those who tried hardest to concentrate, remember and keep going.

Teaching Grammar, Punctuation and Spelling Through Drama

Who will do it?

Learning objective
Active and passive verbs

Preparation
Talk with your pupils about an active verb, which is spoken or written when the subject of a sentence performs an action, and a passive verb, which occurs when an action is done to the subject of a sentence.

Invite the pupils to make cards to represent nouns that could be the subject of a sentence, such as: *boy, girl, man, woman, horse, cow, bag, book, flower, pen, apple* and *sausage*. Ensure that they have one card each and that they are all different.

Make two more different noun cards for yourself and demonstrate the use of active and passive verbs by using them in two sentences that mean the same thing but take one noun and then the other to be the subject. For example: *The rabbit ate the carrot* (active verb – ate). *The carrot was eaten by the rabbit* (passive verb – was eaten by).

Activity
Ask each pupil to decide whether his noun is more likely to perform actions (such as: *girl, boy* or *horse*), or to have actions done to it (such as: *bag, book* or *banana*), and to sit in either the active or the passive group.

Begin with the active group and invite each pupil in turn to walk over to point to a pupil in the passive group, to perform an appropriate action for the two nouns and to state the sentence using an active verb. For example:

> *The man wrote with the pen.*
> or
> *The dog chased the ball.*

Ask the pupils of the passive group then to take turns to walk over to point to a pupil of the active group and state a sentence with a passive verb. The chosen pupil from the active group must then perform the action for his partner, as passive verbs do not perform actions themselves. For example:

> *The banana was picked by the monkey.*
> or
> *The flower was watered by the girl.*

Extension/challenge
Make a list of sentences, some containing active verbs and some containing passive verbs. Invite pupils to sit in spaces and listen carefully as you read out each sentence clearly. As soon as they hear each verb, the pupils should respond by running on the spot if the verb is active and lying on the floor if the verb is passive.

Ensure that the verbs occur in a random order and gradually increase the pace until pupils can no longer keep up and are lying on the floor, laughing.

© Debbie Chalmers and Brilliant Publications

Describe it to me

Learning objective
Adverbs of manner

Preparation
Make equal numbers of cards to represent verbs in the present tense (such as *climb, slide, speak* and *hum*), cards to represent adjectives that take *ly* without a spelling change (such as *cross, sad, quick* and *loud*), and cards to represent the ending *ly*.

Explain to your pupils that adverbs are describing words for verbs and that 'adverbs of manner' answer questions such as: How did that happen? or What was it like?

Activity
Give one card to each pupil and invite them all to walk around, holding up their cards and looking at each other's cards. After a short time, ask them to form suitable groups of three and to put their words in order and act out their phrase together. For example: *run slowly, sing quietly* or *pull strongly*.

Extension/challenge
Divide the pupils into groups of four and ask each group to decide on a verb and think of four different adverbs to describe it. For example: to stamp – *loudly, crossly, quickly* and *slowly*.

After a short period of practice, ask each group in turn to perform their actions while everybody else tries to guess the verb and adverbs that are being described.

© Debbie Chalmers and Brilliant Publications

When was that?

Learning objective

Adverbs of time

Preparation

Invite your pupils to help you to think of time words, such as: *yesterday, today, tomorrow, now, soon, later* and *one day*. Explain that these words are 'adverbs of time' and they describe when something happened, that it is happening or when it will happen.

Make a list of the words for your own use and also write each word onto a separate card for the pupils. (You will need one card per pupil, to represent past, present and future times in roughly equal quantities.)

Activity

Scatter the cards all over the floor and then ask pupils to work together to sort them into the three main bands of time: past, present and future. For example:

Past
last Tuesday
two weeks ago
earlier

Present
now
this morning
immediately

Future
tomorrow night
next year
after lunch

Once they have sorted the cards into the three separate piles, invite the pupils to divide themselves into three groups and sit down with the cards. Talk with them about using adverbs of time with the correct verb tenses. For example: *Yesterday, I went to school. Now I am reading my book. Next weekend, I will go to the cinema.*

Invite each pupil to take one card from the pile and to think of a sentence using that adverb of time, together with a verb of his choice and an appropriate subject or place.

When everybody is ready, ask each pupil in turn to mime his sentence and then to speak it aloud. Those using the present tense are likely to be simpler mimes, while those representing the past or the future may be much more elaborate. For example, to mime the sentence *Yesterday I went to school*, the child might mime: walking to school, opening a bag, taking out a book and a pen, sitting at a desk to write, tidying up, waving to friends, then walking home again.

Extension/challenge

Give each pupil a card representing a different adverb of time and encourage them to discuss and decide together how to sort themselves into a 'time line'. Choose carefully when giving out the adverbs, according to your pupils' ability and confidence levels. All may appear to play equally if some have simpler words, such as: *today, tomorrow* or *next week*, while others face a greater challenge with terms such as: *two weekends ago* or *the first Thursday of next month*.

Where shall we go?

Learning objective
Adverbs of place

Preparation
Talk with your pupils about how to use 'adverbs of place' (such as *here, there, far away, nearby, indoors* or *outside*) to answer the question: Where did it happen?

Create four 'bases', using mats, hoops or chalked squares or circles. Two should be fairly close to each other at one end of the room and two fairly close together at the other end.

Activity
Divide the pupils into four groups and ask one group to stand in each base. Explain that the bases are known as *Here, There, Far away* and *Nearby*, but that they change and swap depending on where a person is standing. Call out the four words, several times each, in a random order and invite pupils to respond to each one as quickly as they can.

When you call *Here!* they freeze where they are; when you call *Nearby!* they jump to the closest base; when you call *Far away!* they run to either of the bases at the other end of the room; when you call *There!* they may move to any of the other three bases.

As all of the pupils are moving around each other or freezing at once, the game becomes very busy.

Extension/challenge
Repeat the game, adding more words to increase the level of difficulty. Create bases to represent: indoors, outside, upstairs, downstairs, at home, away or any other suitable places suggested by pupils, as well as the original four bases. Remember to make them large enough, as all of the pupils may need to stand on some of them at the same time.

Teaching Grammar, Punctuation and Spelling Through Drama

Constructing theories

Learning objective

Connectives/conjunctions – single words

Preparation

Initiate a discussion with your pupils about parts that connect with each other, as in construction kits or jigsaw puzzles. Then talk with them about shorter and longer sentences and explain that longer ones are usually shorter sentences, clauses or phrases joined together by connectives, which may also be called conjunctions.

Ask them to help you to complete some examples, such as:

> You can walk along the wall, but …

Pupils may come up with various ideas, which are all equally valid. For example:

> you must jump off at the end
> you need to balance carefully
> you may not step on the grass

Activity

This is ideally a game for 18–30 players, using six connectives. If you have fewer in your group, play the game twice, using three of the connectives each time.

Invite six pupils to represent the connectives: *and, but, while, although, before* and *after*. Divide the others into two groups of six or more and ask each group, working as individuals or pairs, to think of six short sentences each, involving a verb in a past tense and a place. For example:

> I danced in the hall.
> I was skipping in the garden.
> We washed in the bathroom.
> We were cooking in the kitchen.

Give all of the pupils time to create and practise mimes to fit their words. Those representing the connectives should use an appropriate facial expression, such as smiling, thinking or waiting, and a gesture, such as indicating with a hand, pointing or raising a finger.

Invite the connectives, one by one, to choose and beckon to a sentence from the first group and then to choose and beckon to one from the second group. The first sentence, followed by the connective, followed by the second sentence should mime then speak, while everybody else checks that the new, longer sentence makes sense.

Extension/challenge

Invite pupils to help you to think of other connectives, such as: *so, because, if, as, since, or* and *until.*

Ask them to form groups of three or more and to mime and then speak a sentence using one of the connectives, in turn, for everybody else to watch. For example:

> I ran all the way home so I felt very tired.
> I went for a long walk because I was enjoying the fresh air.

© Debbie Chalmers and Brilliant Publications

All link up

Learning objective
Connectives/conjunctions – two or more words

Preparation
Talk with your pupils about using two or more words together as a connective or conjunction in exactly the same way as a single word.

Make cards to represent short words that can be put together to form connectives. For example: *only, when, if, as, well, in, order, to, however, much, even, though*. (You will need more than one of some of the words.)

Activity
Ask pupils to work together to join the words to make connectives and lay them in a line on the floor, one under the other. For example:

> *only when*
> *only if*
> *as well as*
> *in order to*
> *even though*

Then invite pupils to think of short sentences or phrases, to say them aloud and to run to stand before or after appropriate connectives, until all the spaces are filled.

Invite each pupil in turn to speak and act out his sentence or phrase, filling in the connective yourself between each pair of pupils. For example:

> *I ate some grapes as well as some raspberries.*
> *I could have my dinner only if I moved my books from the table.*

Encourage them to listen carefully to each other, to make the phrases fit together correctly. If they hear a sentence such as:

> *I ate some raspberries as well as I like going outside.*

They should be able to tell that it doesn't sound right or make real sense.

Extension/challenge
Give each pupil or small group a different connective and ask them all to listen carefully while you begin a sentence. Encourage them to try to end the sentence in original ways, using their connectives. Make the opening phrase very simple and general, such as:

> *I like cats...*

Pupils may then suggest endings such as:

> *only when they're asleep*
> *only if they're friendly*
> *as well as guinea pigs*
> *however much they miaow*
> *even though their fur makes a mess on the furniture*

Invite pupils to speak their endings and also act them out symbolically (eg by stroking cats, covering their ears or brushing the sofa).

Opposite ideas

Learning objective
Prefixes to change meaning

Preparation
Make cards to represent prefixes, such as: *un, dis, anti, multi, ex, mis, im, up, down, under, over, turn* and *centi*.

Also make words that can definitely be combined with one or more of the prefixes, such as: *happy, believe, clockwise, coloured, change, understand, patient, stairs, coat* and *metre*.

Activity
Give one card to each pupil and ask them not to show them to each other. Explain that prefixes are added in front of words and that the new beginnings change the meanings of the words. Encourage the pupils with word cards to think of mimes to demonstrate their words, while those with prefix cards imagine the types of words that they might change. Allow a few minutes of silent independent thinking.

Invite the pupils with words to sit in spaces and those with prefixes to wait in a group, keeping their cards hidden from each other. Ask the pupils with words, in turn, each to stand up to mime and then to speak his word. Any pupil who thinks that his prefix would fit with the word may go to join him and call out the new word. The two pupils may then act out the longer word together. For example: a pupil mimes *happy*, is joined by the prefix *un* and they mime *unhappy* together.

If two or three pupils have prefixes that could fit, they may all move as soon as they recognize the match. The words may then be acted out in turn by the pairs. For example: *undercoat, overcoat, turncoat*.

If no prefix goes to a word, ask all of the prefixes to show their cards and encourage pupils to help each other to find one or more that would fit.

Extension/challenge
Invite the pupils to work in pairs. Give each pair a word that could take at least one prefix and ask them to think of a suitable prefix for themselves, then act out the two words for everybody else to watch. They will see that often the words are opposites, as in: *believe/ disbelieve* or *clockwise/anticlockwise*. But, sometimes, a word can be changed completely, as in: *grade/centigrade*.

Allow hyphenated words, such as *part-time* or *self-control*, but use your discretion and knowledge of your pupils' individual needs when choosing whether to accept two words that are used together but not linked or hyphenated, such as *guinea pig*. Strictly speaking, this is a compound word and not a prefix, but, in some cases, it may be a sign that a pupil who was struggling to understand is suddenly beginning to grasp the concept and he should be praised for his contribution. To avoid confusion, more able pupils may work separately on another occasion to explore the subtle differences between types of prefix and compound words.

This way or that way?

Learning objective
Suffixes to change meaning

Preparation
Make a list of suffixes that are used to change the meanings of words, such as: *ness, ment, tion, sion, ive, ist, ice, ess, ent, ant* and *er*. Write the suffixes onto separate cards that can be held up, or onto a white board, one under the other, as a clear list. (Do not write words to go with them. Play the game verbally, to avoid the grammar game turning into a spelling exercise.)

Activity
Hold up or point to one suffix at a time and invite pupils to think of a word that could go before it. The first pupil to say that he has a word may be encouraged to stand up and act it out, then explain it to the group. Some words may only require one act, as the meaning changes very little. For example: *happy* can be a grinning face and *happiness* may be indicated by spreading arms to share the smiles. Others may change the word more obviously and require two acts, such as: *cycle* and *cyclist* or *ignore* and *ignorant*.

Encourage each pupil to take at least one turn and try not to choose the same few pupils too often, but take note of those who are particularly able and confident and consider working with them again separately, as a small group, to develop this task on another occasion.

Extension/challenge
Play the game in the opposite way, by giving the pupils a word and asking them to supply a suffix.

Either sit in a circle and ask each pupil in turn, allowing others to help whenever anybody is stuck, or stick cards representing common suffixes to the walls and then call out words, encouraging pupils to go quickly to touch an appropriate suffix for each one. (You might use: *ness, ment, tion, ess, er, ant, ice* and *ist*.)

Remind pupils that, for some words, there may be more than one perfectly correct answer, such as: *serve – service, servant* and *server*.

Different forms

Learning objective

Suffixes to change tense or type of word

Preparation

Make a list of verbs that take the suffixes *ing, ed* and *er*, such as: *roll, skip, climb* and *dance*. Avoid those which change in the past tense, such as *run, sing* and *think*. Keep the list for your own use and play the game verbally, so that differences in spellings don't distract pupils from the grammar concept.

Activity

Divide the pupils into groups of four. Explain that each group will have a root verb and will act out the word alone, the word with the suffix *ing*, the word with the suffix *ed* and the word with the suffix *er*, demonstrating how the verb moves through the present tense or into the past tense or becomes a noun.

Give a different verb to each group and invite them all to prepare their acts. For example: the first actor might represent *roll* by rolling over and back once; the second actor might roll around the floor continuously to represent *rolling*, the third actor might roll away into the distance and then stop to demonstrate *rolled*, while the fourth actor might lie on the floor with arms and legs stretched into a long thin shape to pretend to be a *roller*.

Other verbs could be demonstrated in a similar way, with three actors performing actions and then the fourth actor striking a pose as a *climber* or a *dancer* and freezing while the others point to him. Pupils may know that a *skipper* works on a ship and create an interesting mime for him after skipping around to illustrate the various tenses of *skip*.

Extension/challenge

Invite pupils to think of words that have more than one meaning, as a root verb or in one of the tenses or as a noun, and to work together to act out the four parts as before, adding extra acts wherever possible. They may need some help with ideas at first.

For example: *wash* (body, clothes, car), *washing* (scrubbing plates and dishes, loading clothes into a washing machine, hanging items up on a line), *washed* (lifting items out of water, drying with a towel, spraying hair with a shower) and *washer* (being a washing machine or a dishwasher).

Also try: *squash* (crush with fist, squeeze together, have a drink), *squashing* (pressing down, pushing together), *squashed* (a flat or crooked shape, squeezing or huddling into a corner), *squasher* (a car crusher or other similar machine). *Stamp* works well too, as you can bang with the feet, authorize papers with a hand tool and stick stamps onto letters.

Who's it?

Learning objective
Pronouns – to replace nouns

Preparation
Make cards to represent common singular nouns, including *a* or *an* before each one. For example: *a tree, a house, a car, a pencil, an elephant, a cat, a book, a table, a chair, an apple, an orange, a biscuit, a cake* and *a bicycle*. Make an equal number of cards to represent the word *it*.

Also make cards to represent appropriate verbs and prepositions in the past tense, to accompany the nouns. For example: *stood under, lived in, sat inside* and *wrote with*.

Ask each pupil to make his own name on one card and either *He* or *She* on another card (with the capital letters, as they will be at the beginnings of sentences). Explain the three singular personal pronouns that can replace people or objects: *he, she* and *it*.

Activity
Divide the pupils into five groups. Invite the first group to hold their name cards, the second group to have *it* cards and the third group to have the verbs and prepositions. The fourth and fifth groups will be smaller, as they will represent *He* and *She*, according to the numbers of boys and girls playing the game.

Ask the *He, She* and *it* groups to wait while the words find each other and stand together to form sentences, such as:
> *David stood under a tree* or
> *Debbie looked at an elephant.*

When all of the sentences are formed, invite the nouns to mime feeling tired and to look around for help. Encourage the pronouns to hurry to replace them, shake hands and stand to attention in the correct places in the sentences, while the nouns wander away and pretend to go to sleep. The sentences will now become:
> *He stood under it* or
> *She looked at it,* etc.

Extension/challenge
Give one common noun card to each pupil and ask him to keep the word a secret from everybody else and to think of a clue to help others guess what it is, using a pronoun to represent himself and one or more verbs, prepositions and places, etc. For example:
> *He writes with it at school* or
> *She sits at it to eat dinner.*

Invite pupils to sit in a group to watch each other and to stand up in turn to speak their clues clearly, accompanying them with a short mime. As soon as somebody guesses the noun, he may jump up and say the whole sentence, including the pupil's name. For example:
> *Andy writes with a pencil at school* or
> *Tess sits at a table to eat dinner.*

His or hers?

Learning objective
Pronouns – singular or plural and possessive

Preparation
Talk with your pupils about the different personal pronouns: first person singular and plural – *I* and *we*, second person singular and plural – both *you*, and third person singular and plural – *he, she, it* and *they*. Also discuss the possessive pronouns that match them: *my, our, your, his, her, its* and *their*.

Activity
Invite pupils to stand in spaces to play a game. Call out pronouns at random and encourage pupils to respond quickly. When you call *I*, they should point to themselves; when you call *we*, they should find a partner. When you call *you*, they may point to one other person or several other people. When you call *he* or *she*, they should point to a boy or a girl; when you call *it*, they should point to the floor, the wall, the window or an object; when you call *they*, pupils should all find partners and point to other pairs.

Once the pupils can play this game confidently, introduce a similar game using the matching possessive pronouns. Give each pupil a folded sheet of paper and ask them to pretend that it is a book.

When you call *my book*, they keep the papers for themselves; when you call *our books*, they form pairs and share the papers. When you call *your book*, each pupil swaps the paper with another person; when you call *your books*, they form pairs and swap with two other people. (This is an added challenge which was not present in the first game and demands careful listening.) When you call *his book* or *her book*, they hand the paper to another boy or girl; when you call *its book*, they throw the papers onto the floor. When you call *their books*, they form two large groups and then each swap a paper with somebody in the other group. (Calling *his book* or *her book* leaves half of the pupils without a paper, so always follow it with *its book*, so that everybody can then pick up one from the floor and continue the game.)

This is fairly complicated and adults may need to demonstrate and support these concepts and remind pupils of the actions until enough of them grasp the idea and can remember quickly. Once they are confident, this game becomes a favourite.

Extension/challenge
Divide the pupils into groups of six (mixed boys and girls). Ask each group to decide on a pretend prop, such as a ball, a pen, a bag or a hat, and to prepare an act to demonstrate the six possessive pronouns: *mine, yours, ours, his, hers* and *theirs*.

For example: one pupil could hold the 'ball' and say *It's mine*, then throw it to another pupil, saying *No, it's yours*. That person may pass it on to a boy, saying, *It's his*, and he may pass it to a girl, saying *No, it's hers*. Three pupils may then stand together as the girl throws it to them, saying *It's theirs*. Finally, all six pupils could stand together, pretending to hold up the 'ball' and say *It's ours!*

Combining words

Learning objective
Compound adjectives – using hyphens

Preparation
Discuss adjectives with your pupils and how it is possible to use two words together to describe a noun, hyphenating them and calling them compound adjectives. Offer some examples, such as: *long-legged*, *three-sided* and *well-known*, and ask them to help to think of others. Write each word on a separate card.

Activity
Give one card to each pupil and ask them all to move around the room, looking at each other's cards and finding as many partners as they can, one after the other. Each time two pupils put their cards together to make a compound adjective, they should act out the word, then separate again to find new partners.

For example: *long-haired, long-legged, three-legged, three-wheeled, three-sided, dog-mad, hopping-mad, mad-looking, good-looking, cross-looking, cross-eyed, well-behaved, well-known.*

Some words will be easier to act out than others, but encourage originality and inventiveness! The more interesting and entertaining the mimes, the more likely it is that pupils will remember the words when they need them for their creative writing.

Extension/challenge
Divide the pupils into groups of three or four. Give each group a different word and challenge them to think of a different compound adjective for each member, using the word as either half. For example: *light* could become *light-headed, light-footed, light-fingered* and *light-hearted*; *sweet* could become *sweet-smelling, sweet-tasting, sweet-tempered* and *bitter-sweet.*

Teaching Grammar, Punctuation and Spelling Through Drama

Where are you now?

Learning objective
Prepositions – relative positions

Preparation
Invite your pupils to stand in one long line facing you. Introduce them to the idea that they are each next to or beside somebody else. Ask each pupil in turn to take his cue and name the person beside him, saying: *I am next to Vicky, I am standing beside Greg*, or something similar. Explain that *next to* and *beside* are prepositions, because prepositions placed in front of nouns or pronouns describe the position of somebody or something in relation to somebody or something else.

Now ask the pupils to make a quarter turn to their left, to stand in a queue, and to describe their positions in turn, saying for example: *I am behind Tess and in front of Andy.* (You or another adult will need to stand at each end of the queue, to ensure that every pupil has somebody both in front of and behind him. Remind pupils that *in front of* and *behind* are also prepositions.

Activity
Divide the pupils into groups of five or six. Give a different noun to each group and invite them to think of an appropriate preposition for each group member that can be acted out to show to everybody else. They could end their performance by speaking the actions aloud, or invite their audience to do so for them.

For example: a group with the word *chair* could sit *on* the chair, hide *under* the chair, jump *over* the chair, stand *beside* the chair, wait *in front of* the chair and skip *around* the chair.

Talk through the actions after each group has finished, saying, for example: So, *you sat on it, hid under it, jumped over it, stood beside it, waited in front of it* and *skipped around it*. This will ensure that all pupils understand that prepositions work in exactly the same way with pronouns, such as *it*, as they do with nouns. It will also offer practice with tenses, as they listen to you changing each verb from present tense to past tense as you describe what you saw.

Extension/challenge
Invite pupils to work in pairs or groups of three to create sentences containing two nouns, one verb (in the present or the past tense) and one preposition, to say them aloud and then to act them out for the rest of the group to watch.

For example:
> *The worm crawls through the tunnel.*
> *The car drives along the road.*
> *The train rushes past the station.*
> *The cat sat under the table.*
> *The man climbed up the mountain.*
> *The fox ran between the trees.*

Say it carefully

Learning objective
Word order – for meaning

Preparation
Make cards to represent equal numbers of verbs (in the past tense), adjectives, prepositions, the word *the* and short speeches (with correct inverted commas, capital letter and any necessary question mark or exclamation mark included) and then twice as many nouns. Explain to your pupils that some words can be moved around within sentences without changing their meanings or making nonsense, but others can't.

Activity
Divide the pupils into groups of six and give to each group: two nouns, one verb, one adjective, one preposition and one speech. Also give them some spare cards and a marker pen, so that they may write any other small connecting words that they need, such as: *to* or *and*. Ask each group to make up a sentence with their words, such as:

> *'Time to go' called Mum through the closed doors.* or
> *Zookeepers shouted to the monkeys 'Find the hidden bananas!'*

(Don't worry about adding extra punctuation outside the speech marks to make the sentences perfectly correct, as they are short enough to manage without and this game concentrates on the order of the words, not commas and colons.)

Invite pupils to continue the activity within their groups, making as many correct sentences as they can with their words. For example:

> *Timmy said "Jump up high" to the brown dog.*
> *"Jump up high" said Timmy to the brown dog.*
> *To the brown dog Timmy said "Jump up high."*

They should hear that the words sound equally good in some different orders, but that some orders sound more awkward and not quite right.

Ask pupils to make a nonsense sentence with their words, such as:

> *"Jump up high" said the dog to brown Timmy.*
> or
> *Said the dog to "Jump up high" Timmy brown.*

Decide together which still work as sentences (as the first example) and which don't mean anything at all (as the second example). They will then see that the structure of a sentence is as important as its words.

Extension/challenge
Invite each pupil to think of an adverb and to create a simple sentence, putting the adverb at the end. For example: *I ran home quickly.*

Ask each pupil then to find a partner and encourage them to change each other's sentences, by moving the adverb to the beginning. For example: *Quickly, I ran home.* They should understand that this doesn't change the meaning of the sentence.

You might choose to discuss with some pupils the similarities between this and the use of an active or a passive verb to describe the same action or event.

Be my partner

Learning objective
Clauses that work alone but may be joined

Preparation
Make cards to represent subjects and verbs that work together and invite your pupils to create clauses using them. Explain that clauses are groups of words that form sentences or parts of sentences. They must always have both a subject and a verb.

Activity
Divide the pupils into two groups. Invite the first group to create clauses using nouns and the second group to create other clauses using pronouns. Ask the pupils of the first group, one by one, to mime their clauses and then speak them aloud. After each one, any member of the second group who thinks that his clause could fit with the one he has just heard should go to join with the speaker to try it out. They may decide on an appropriate connective together.

They may create sentences such as:
The lion roared and he was afraid.
The sun shone so we went for a walk.
The woman bought some shoes when she went into town on the bus.

Extension/challenge
Challenge pupils to join up three or four clauses with various connectives to make longer sentences, such as:
The sun shone and the wind blew, so we went for a walk but we wore our coats.

They will need to work together to discuss and negotiate ideas, develop themes and suggest and agree on suitable connectives.

The lion roared

and they were afraid.

© Debbie Chalmers and Brilliant Publications

Lift us out

Learning objective
Subordinate clauses

Preparation
Initiate a discussion with your pupils about complex sentences with more than one clause, such as:

The playground is great on a fine day, and the slide is our favourite as long as it's dry, but the equipment can be very slippery when it's raining.

We must do our homework tonight, even if we don't feel like it, because we have to hand it in tomorrow.

Write down each of the three clauses for each sentence on separate cards. Invite pupils to lay them out on the floor and read them, then to lift out the middle clause, push the other two together and read the sentence again. They will see that this makes a sentence with only two clauses, that is less interesting but still correct. Explain that the middle clause is called the subordinate clause, because it is less important than the other two, since the sentence can exist without it but not without either of the other two clauses.

Activity
Divide the pupils into groups of five and ask each group to create a sentence containing three clauses. They should check it carefully to ensure that the subordinate (middle) clause can be lifted out and taken away, leaving two clauses that still make sense together. (You may offer some pupils the clue that the first clause would usually begin with a subject and the second and third clauses with a connective or a verb.)

Once they have created a sentence together, three of the pupils should represent the separate clauses and two pupils should represent commas. Invite each group in turn to present their sentence to everybody else. One pupil should speak the first clause, then a comma may crawl up beside him, the next pupil should speak the second clause, the other comma may crawl up beside him and then the last pupil should speak the third clause. When the whole sentence has been presented, the two commas may jump up and run away with the subordinate (second) clause. The two pupils who are left should then speak the first and third clauses again as a shorter sentence.

Possible sentences might be:

The boy climbed the hill, where the sun shone brightly, and soon felt too hot.

The cats sat on the wall, swishing their tails, to sing in the moonlight.

Extension/challenge
Invite pupils to experiment with two and three clause sentences in which the subordinate clause doesn't appear in the middle between two commas. Groups of three and four pupils may create sentences such as:

I'm going into town after work today, so I might look for a new coat.

We did go to the party, because it was raising money for a good cause, although the girl we don't like was one of the organizers.

In these examples, the last clause is subordinate and could be lifted away from the sentence.

Excuse me

Learning objective

Degrees of formality – strangers, requests, complaints, occasions and events

Preparation

Discuss with your pupils the types of people and situations for which it would be appropriate to use very formal language, such as when communicating with strangers. They could be speaking to a person directly or over the telephone, or composing and sending letters or e-mails.

Suggest suitable greetings to begin and end conversations or correspondence and the types of words that should and should not be included. There will be no apostrophes used within words to form contractions, no slang or colloquial speech and no 'chatting'. Politeness must be paramount and clear questions and answers, requests, directions, orders or complaints given, either verbally or in writing, and kept short and relevant.

Ensure that pupils understand basic rules and traditions, such as writing *Sir/Madam* to a stranger and ending with *Yours faithfully*, but using a person's name if possible and ending with *Yours sincerely*. It is usual, when speaking to a person, especially on the telephone, to use an opening statement such as *Good morning Madam* or to attract the attention of a stranger by saying *Excuse me Sir*. At the end of a formal conversation, you might say *I am sorry to have disturbed you*, *Thank you for your time* or *Thank you very much for your help*, depending on the circumstances.

Activity

Invite the pupils to work in pairs. Ask one third of the pairs to pretend that one is formally interviewing the other for a job. Ask another third to pretend that one is making a telephone call to the other to try to sell him a product or some insurance. Ask the final third to pretend that one has written a complaint and the other has replied to it (politely). If possible, ask another adult to assist you in giving a demonstration of each of the three scenarios, to offer pupils some ideas to work from.

Allow the pupils time to prepare and practise their role-plays, then invite them to show them to each other. (The third group should pretend to be reading their letters aloud.) When each pair has performed, offer constructive criticism and invite other pupils to make comments and suggestions for improvement. Encourage them all to gradually develop their abilities to do this in a kind and supportive manner. Repeat the activity on several occasions, allowing pupils to take on different roles and to try out the ideas and suggestions.

Extension/challenge

Talk about the importance of body language and clear enunciation when speaking and of clarity and correct spelling, punctuation and grammar when writing. Invite pupils to include a few deliberate errors in their role-plays, such as fidgeting, muttering or pronouncing somebody's name wrongly, and challenge their audience to spot them quickly and call out reminders and corrections.

Quite correct

Learning objective
Degrees of formality – school, books and essays

Preparation
Explain that the correct form of written and spoken English, used in schools and business, books and magazines, essays and articles, government and law, is known as Standard English. Whichever other languages or dialects we may speak when abroad, in the course of our work or when with our own families and friends, we must also learn to use Standard English correctly in order to communicate effectively and to command full recognition and respect as British citizens.

Activity
Ask each pupil to choose a partner and ask, within each pair, one to be a student and the other to be a teacher. Invite the 'students' to invent scenarios. They may decide, for example, to ask a question about class work, to explain why they haven't finished their homework, to ask permission to fetch a book or to admit that they've forgotten to bring their kit. Ask the 'teachers' to respond to them appropriately.

Conversations between people who know each other quite well but who are placed in a situation of one having authority over the other, particularly within an establishment such as a school or an office, will include less formal language than that used by strangers. Some contractions and expressions that occur within the local dialect may be acceptable and the tone will be generally more friendly. However, impress upon pupils that polite speech, good manners, a respectful tone, honesty and listening to each other are vital and support them in becoming confident in their use of these. *Excuse me Miss, Please Sir* or *Thank you for helping me* can ensure a successful conversation and a constructive relationship, as can *I appreciate you telling me the truth* or *I'm glad you asked for help when you didn't understand.*

Encourage the pupils to swap roles and repeat the exercise.

Extension/challenge
Ask each pupil to choose a topic that they know lots about. It may be a hobby (such as swimming, dancing, gymnastics or football), keeping a pet animal (such as a cat, dog, hamster or tortoise) or a place they visit regularly (such as a park, wood, beach or shop).

Invite them each to prepare a description that could be included within a non-fiction book or a magazine, using Standard English. For example, it might say: *The beach has soft, golden sand and several types of crab can be found there, living in the rock pools.* It would not state: *The sand's nice and soft down there, where all them crabs crawl out of the water!*

Or try a report on an event, such as a swimming gala. It would be correct to say: *The green team were the champions, winning five of the eight races, while the other three teams won only one each.* It would not be appropriate to state: *It was five times that green team came first and the others weren't much good!*

Familiarity

Learning objective
Degrees of formality – home, family and friends

Preparation
Ask each pupil to imagine the way he speaks when he is with members of his own family or close friends. Discuss the fact that it will almost definitely include some particular expressions and similes that may not be used or understood outside his social circle or in another part of the country. Explain that informal speech, that is often used by people in their daily lives, may be known as Nonstandard English. It may include slang, shortened words, nicknames and dialects. This type of speech may also appear in written dialogues and scripts to allow characters to speak as real people. If we come across it when acting or reading aloud, we must imagine the way the character would have spoken and try to approximate his voice, accent, expressions and dialect.

Find two unused or turned-off telephones and a sheet of paper to be used as props for the extension activity.

Activity
Invite the pupils to form pairs or groups of three. Ask each group to prepare a role-play scenario in which a child asks his parent(s) or carer(s) for something he really wants. They may say yes or no but the important part of the activity is the way they speak to each other. Despite the 'child' trying to 'be good' in order to get his own way and despite the 'adult(s)' possibly feeling annoyed or worried, there should be a familiarity and a confidence demonstrated through phrases such as:

What do you want that for?

Just because the boy next door's got one?
What about all the stuff you had for your birthday?

and

Oh go on, please!
You know how much I want one.
If you get me one, I'll help you tidy up every day and I'll clean the car!

Extension/challenge
Divide the pupils into two groups. Give a telephone to one pupil in each group and invite the pair to spontaneously create a conversation between two friends who are arranging to meet up and do something together. For example:

Hi, it's me!
Hello, what's happening this weekend?
Do you want to go out on Saturday? To that new place?
All right, if you like. Is it expensive, though?
Not too bad, but you have to dress up a bit.
Wear your jacket like mine then and let's wear our boots.

Pass the telephones around and encourage all pupils to take a turn at the activity.

Extend this further by imagining a letter or email written to a sibling or cousin, describing an event. Invite one pupil at a time to hold a sheet of paper and pretend to 'read out' the letter or email he has received. For example:

It was so cool! Loads of people and loud music and flashing lights. Mum and Dad would've hated it! You must come next time.

Could you tell me?

Learning objective
Asking and answering questions

Preparation
Make cards to represent all of the most common types of question – Who? What? Where? When? Why? How? – and stick them onto the walls. Discuss the meaning of each with your pupils, explaining that not every question contains one of these actual words but that many of them could include one. A good way of checking whether a sentence is a statement or a question is to try thinking of the six words and deciding if one of them would be substituted for some of the words. Also, remind them that a question always invites or requests a verbal response (or a sign, such as a nod).

Activity
Call out questions and encourage the pupils to move quickly to stand beside the relevant question word for each one. At random points, include a sentence that is not a question. Ask pupils to sit down on the floor in the middle of the room if they hear one of these. Typical questions might be:

Which one is your teacher? (Who?)
Is that a fruit? (What?)
Is their house far away? (Where?)
Did you get home late yesterday? (When?)
Did something make her do that? (Why?)
Is there a way to make it easier? (How?)

Their dog barks during the night is just a statement, but *Is there a reason for their dog barking during the night?* is a Why? question. Listen for the difference in inflection.

Extension/challenge
There are also 'checking-up' questions, such as:
Did you finish your essay?
Are you going to the party tomorrow?

Would you be able to let me know by this afternoon?
Can you help me with lunch?
Will you remember to hand in your homework?

And there are negative forms of most questions, such as:
Didn't you finish your essay?
Aren't you going to the party?

Sometimes, we use a question to confirm what we already know, or to answer a question put to us. For example:
So that's fine, isn't it?
You like that, don't you?
You won't forget, will you?
I said so, didn't I?

Invite pupils to work in pairs to create and prepare a short dialogue that is full of these questions. For example:
Did you finish your work?
Yes, so that's fine, isn't it?
Then can you come to my party tomorrow?
I don't know yet, do I?
Will you be able to let me know by this afternoon?
Yes, I said that, didn't I?

Explain that, in English, a verb is chosen to agree with the sentence when creating a question in this way. (In some other languages, eg French, it is possible to change a statement to a question by adding a phrase meaning *Is it not so?* to the end.) In English, a question mark must always be written at the end.

Do as I say

Learning objective
Giving orders and commands

Preparation
Play a game involving giving instructions, orders and commands, such as *Simon says*. Invite the pupils to take turns to be the leader. Encourage them to understand that an order or command requests a response that may be verbal or physical. Suggest that, if the sentence would make sense with the words *You must* at the beginning, it is probably an order or a command, or at least an instruction.

Activity
Divide the pupils into two equal groups. Invite members of the first group to perform actions (or inactions) of their choice, simultaneously. One may hop, one may skip, one may crawl, one may freeze, etc. Ask each member of the second group to go to one member of the first group and order them to stop. For example:

> *Stop hopping!*
> *No skipping here!*
> *You must not jump any more!*
> *Stop crawling at once!*

Now ask the second group to stand in spaces and invite each member of the first group to give a command for one of them to follow. For example:

> *Come over here to me!*
> *Go to the other side of the room!*
> *Sit down and be very quiet!*
> *Balance on one leg for ten seconds!*

Suggest that they may include some commands that require verbal responses, such as:

> *Tell me your name!*
> *Count to twenty!*
> *Sing a song!*
> *Tell me a joke!*

Extension/challenge
Invite the pupils to form groups of three and play a game to compare statements, questions and commands. Ask each group to choose a sentence and adapt it to be a question, a command and a statement, then deliver it as a short role-play sequence, with actions and expressions.

A typical script might be:
Father:　*Are you going to bed?*
Child:　*No, not yet.*
Mother:　*Go to bed now!*
Child:　*I'm going to bed!*

Try repeating the sequences using very polite speech, to show that good manners can turn both statements and commands into questions, but that they must still be obeyed.

An example of this might be:
Teacher:　*Would you all sit down over here?*
Children:　*May we sit on the carpet, please?*
Teacher:　*Could you please look this way?*
Children:　*Do we need to look at the board, Miss?*
Teacher:　*Will you please stop talking and listen now?*

Break it down

Learning objective
Using paragraphs

Preparation
Provide a selection of fiction books for your pupils to look through. Draw their attention to the paragraphs on each page and ask them to imagine how much more difficult it might be to read the text if it wasn't broken down into any sections at all. It would be quite daunting to read whole pages without a pause and hard to find your place whenever you returned after a break. Explain that each paragraph deals with a separate idea.

Activity
Decide on a character or a theme for a story that you know will appeal to your pupils. A small group of pupils may work individually, but, if your group is large, ask them to work in pairs or threes. Announce the story – for example: *A Dog's Busy Day*. Invite each pupil, pair or group to think of one idea connected to the title and to create an act or mime which they can perform to everybody else. When all of the acts have been performed, work together to put them into a logical sequence. For example:

> *The dog woke up, stretched and looked around; he felt hungry and went into the kitchen for breakfast; he ran out into the garden and ran around in circles; his owner called and he went out for a walk; he tried to chase a cat, but it ran up a tree; he barked at a squirrel when it ran past him; he jumped in puddles and then shook himself dry; he sniffed at hedgehogs under the bushes; he came home and chewed his bone; he fell asleep in his basket.*

Each of the short acts becomes one scene within the sequence. If the actors stand in order, leaving small gaps between them, they can represent the separate paragraphs of the story.

Your stories are likely to be much more exciting and varied than this and it may take some imaginative skills to include all of the pupils' separate ideas in one story, but enlist their help and accept fairly vague links if they are happy with them!

Extension/challenge
Invite the pupils to sit in a circle and tell a story together. Begin with a well-known story, such as a class favourite or a fairy tale. Ask each person in turn to tell a short part of the story and stop at an appropriate point, such as after an event. The next person should take his cue each time and continue the story with the next new idea.

Suggest that each pupil links an arm with the previous pupil as he finishes his speech, to indicate that the separate paragraphs link together to make a whole story. When the last arms are linked and the circle is complete, the story should end. You may choose to have an adult as the last person to speak, adding as much or as little as necessary to bring the story to a satisfactory conclusion.

Taller than some

Learning objective
Full stops and capital letters to make sentences

Preparation
Make a large collection of word cards, including nouns, verbs, connectives/conjunctions and prepositions, so that a variety of sentences may be formed. Ensure that the intended sentences are simple and obvious enough to be recognized quickly. They will probably have four, five or six words. For example:

> *The girl sang a song.*
> *Boys like burgers for lunch.*

Also make a number of cards with large dots on them, to represent full stops.

Activity
Give one card to each pupil. There should be at least one full stop for each six words. Ask the pupils to move around, reading each other's words and working together to create sentences by standing in lines so that the words read from left to right. Whenever a group forms a sentence, they should call for a full stop and a pupil with that card can run to stand at the end of the line.

As soon as a sentence is completed by a full stop, the pupil with the first word must hold it up higher to show that it now needs a capital letter. Ask two or more sentences to make a longer line by standing next to each other, ensuring that the pupils notice the capital letter after each full stop.

Sentences may be funny or nonsense, as long as the word order and punctuation is correct and they may be read aloud and understood.

Extension/challenge
Include some names and other proper nouns, that must always have a capital letter, such as Christmas, Diwali and England.

Remind pupils to always hold these words high, wherever they appear, and to remember that the first word of a sentence must have a capital letter as well as any proper nouns, so that there may be more than one in a sentence.

© Debbie Chalmers and Brilliant Publications

May I ask you?

Learning objective
Using question marks

Preparation
Talk with your pupils about sentences and questions and encourage them to look at books and other texts and to spot questions by recognizing the question marks at the ends of them.

Invite each pupil to draw a large question mark on a square of card for his own use.

Activity
Ask the pupils to sit in spaces on the floor and to practise listening for the differences between questions and other sentences, as you say them aloud. Offer a range of sentences with questions mixed into them at random. For example:

> *I saw a mouse. Did you see a mouse? Shall we go to the shops? The shops will shut soon. I hope the car will start. Do you think the car will start? What do you need to buy? Let's get some sausages for dinner.*

Remind them to listen for the differences in inflection as you speak. A voice usually rises towards the end when asking a question, but should stay on the level or gradually become lower during most other types of sentence.

Ask pupils to hold up their question mark cards every time they hear a question and then to put them down on the floor again. Once they are confident, ask them to listen to your sentences and then stand up with their cards and turn them into questions.

For example:

You say:	*I have a blue car.*
Pupils say:	*Do you have a blue car?*
You say:	*It's time for lunch.*
Pupils say:	*Is it time for lunch?*

They may do this individually, in turn, or as a group, in unison.

Extension/challenge
Invite the pupils to stand in a line to listen to the person on their left and then speak to the person on their right. Take the first position in the line yourself and make a statement, then ask a question. Each pupil in turn should answer a question, add a statement and then ask a question.
For example:

> *I am English. Are you English?*
> *No, I am Japanese. I am a girl. Are you a girl?*
> *No, I am a boy. I like cheese. Do you like cheese?*
> *Yes, I like cheese. I bring a packed lunch to school. Do you bring a packed lunch?*

Each time a pupil asks a question, he must hold up his question mark card.

How amazing!

Learning objective
Using exclamation marks

Preparation
Provide a selection of picture books that include sentences and phrases with exclamation marks and also some books with more text, both fiction and non-fiction. Encourage your pupils to search for exclamation marks within the books and to decide when they are used. (This may be when something is exciting, very funny, scary, surprising, unexpected or impressive, or in speeches to indicate that a character is cross or shouting.) Ensure that they notice that only one exclamation mark is used at a time and it is always enough. More than one is incorrect. It 'screams' at the reader and distracts from the true meaning and purpose of the writing.

Activity
Divide the pupils into small groups (of three to six members). Invite them to become explorers reporting their finds to television cameras. They may choose to explore a jungle, desert, forest, arctic waste, island, mountain, shipwreck, or any exciting place.

Invite each group to prepare a speech, with acting, to perform to everybody else. The finds should be as imaginative and amusing as possible and certainly don't need to be true. Each time they report something worthy of an exclamation mark, they should all make a star jump into the air, but they must be careful not to over-use them and to build up information before imparting each surprising, scary or impressive fact.

For example, a group in the jungle might report:

We've travelled all night on tiptoe just to creep up on a red-headed, yellow-legged, sticky-backed frog. It's so tiny that it's hard to see it and its camouflage hides it in the leaves of this plant. There may even be six million of them watching us from this one plant right now! We'll just look at them quietly and not disturb them. Under the plant, live deadly snakes with very good hearing, even though they don't have any ears. They can hear people coming from a thousand miles away! They only bite if they're hungry, so we have to hope they're not today. They could be asleep. But, if they did bite one of us, the poison could kill in two and a half seconds! So, there would be no point in getting the first aid kit out for that!

Extension/challenge
Invite groups of pupils to create cartoon or comedy stories in the same way. It is harder to think up fictional humour than pretend amazing facts, but they may use 'silent movie' type humour and combine mimes with speeches. Encourage them to build up to exclamation marks, rather than to use them too soon. Slipping on a banana skin and falling over is only mildly amusing. Slipping on some leaves, bumping into a tree and dislodging a coconut, which falls down onto the handle of a knife, which jerks upwards and happens to fall down again neatly slicing a banana in two would probably be worthy of an exclamation mark!

© Debbie Chalmers and Brilliant Publications

Find the links

Learning objective
Commas to divide clauses

Preparation
Make a number of cards to represent commas, a slightly smaller number of cards to represent full stops and a smaller number depicting the word *and*. Also make cards which show short phrases/clauses. For example:

> *dogs were barking*
> *rain fell steadily*
> *everything outside was silent*

Activity
Give one card to each pupil. Invite the commas to crawl between two clauses and link arms to join them together. Ask three or more clauses to combine to make a sentence, with commas between them, and invite an *and* to walk between the last two, instead of a comma. Encourage a full stop to jump to the end and then ask for the first phrase to be held up higher to show that it now needs a capital letter.

Extension/challenge
Ask the commas and the *and* words to create longer and more complex sentences by combining large numbers of clauses through crawling into the right places between them and joining them by linking arms.

Make a rule that each group of linked clauses must be related enough to make a fairly sensible sentence, not a collection of random nonsense.

Teaching Grammar, Punctuation and Spelling Through Drama
© Debbie Chalmers and Brilliant Publications

Wait a moment

Learning objective

Commas to create pauses for reading aloud

Preparation

Make up some very short stories or paragraphs, full of fairly obvious dramatic pauses, for your pupils to read aloud. Type them using a clear, large font and print them out. Spooky and scary stories work well if the group enjoys fiction. If the pupils prefer non-fiction, try using descriptions of performing a task, hobby or stunt or having an adventure.

Activity

Gather the pupils together as a group and give out stories to those who are able and willing to read aloud. Allow them a few minutes to practise, while explaining to the other pupils that they will represent the commas.

Ask pupils to take turns to read out stories, as slowly and clearly as possible. Encourage the group to jump up, turn around and sit down again every time they think that there should be a comma to create a short pause.

Extension/challenge

Ask the commas to sit in a line or a circle, rather than a group, and to take turns to jump up individually when they feel that the next comma is needed. This requires each pupil to listen and think individually, rather than just copying the group or following somebody else. It also prevents the same pupils from leading throughout the activity, making it easier to tell who has grasped the concept confidently and who might still be struggling with it.

However, do let others of the group call out to help a pupil who cannot decide when to jump up, rather than allowing embarrassment or under-confidence to spoil the enjoyment of the activity.

© Debbie Chalmers and Brilliant Publications

Keep us apart

Learning objective

Commas to separate items within a list

Preparation

Think of possible collections of objects or concepts, such as fruit, vegetables, movements, weather, animals, mini-beasts, shapes and vehicles. Make lists of examples for each one and keep them as notes, in case your pupils need suggestions or prompts. Decide in advance which themes would be most suitable for particular groups of pupils. Animals, mini-beasts or movements are much easier to mime than fruits, vegetables or vehicles, but it can be much more fun for confident and experienced pupils to try to guess banana, onion or taxi . (Be aware that certain themes that sound simple, such as colours, may be almost impossible to act out.)

Activity

Divide the pupils into groups of seven or more, give each group a different theme and ask them to make a list of relevant items that they can act out or mime. Explain that different members of the group need to represent at least four nouns with two commas and the word *and*. For example: *cats, dogs, monkeys and elephants* or *jumping, hopping, dancing and jogging*. The nouns should mime or act out the words, while the commas and the *and* should join them together by linking arms.

Ask each group to perform to the others and invite them to guess the nouns that are being acted.

Extension/challenge

Ask the whole group to make one big list in the same way, with half of the pupils representing nouns and the other half representing commas that crawl between the words and link arms to join them together. Then invite them to swap roles and do it again. Remember to ask one different pupil each time to represent the word *and*.

Chant the lists aloud together, pausing slightly at each comma. Explain that these are lists, not sentences, and so they do not yet have capital letters or full stops, but that they could be found within sentences.

Ready to speak?

Learning objective
Commas in complex sentences and speeches

Preparation
Create a fairly long sentence and write out the phrases/clauses on long cards and a selection of interchangeable names, ages and occupations on separate smaller cards. Also make a number of cards depicting commas.

Activity
Give one card to each pupil. Encourage pupils to form small groups by enclosing a name, age or occupation between two commas and then to fit themselves between clauses to form complex sentences. For example:

She saw her neighbour, Margaret, in the garden with her new puppy, six months old, and remembered to tell her friend, the baker, when she went out to the shops.

Extension/challenge
Invite some pupils to each choose a character, such as a police officer or an old lady or gentleman, and to imagine a scenario, such as a minor car collision or the opening of a concert. Choose others to be narrators and others to be commas.

Ask the pupils to form groups of narrator, comma and character and to prepare to perform their speech to the rest of the group. They might have the character speaking, then the comma crawling in beside him and then the narrator saying something such as *said the man angrily*. Or they might have the narrator beginning with a speech such as *The conductor bowed to the audience and announced*, then the comma jumping in beside him and then the character giving his speech.

That one's mine

Learning objective
Apostrophes to indicate possession

Preparation
Ask each pupil to make his own name and a noun of his choice (such as: *car, dog, house, book* or *bicycle*) on separate cards. Make lots of cards representing apostrophes and lots of cards representing the letter *s* and put them into two piles on the floor.

Activity
Explain to the pupils that the aim of the game is to collect four cards to make a clause, such as: *Vicky's sandwich* or *Andy's drink*. The rules are that each player must collect an apostrophe card and an *s* card from the piles and swap his name card with another player and his noun card with a different player. These tasks may be completed in any order.

Countdown: 3-2-1-go! and encourage pupils to collect cards and swap them with each other, until everybody has a completed clause. Then ask the pupils to speak their clauses aloud, in turn.

Challenge the pupils to think, read, speak and play the game more quickly by giving them a time limit of either seconds counted aloud or the length of one song played on a CD.

Remind pupils never to use an apostrophe when adding *s* just to create a plural word!

(Warn them that some adults do not always get this right and they may well see this particular mistake in shops and magazines, but that they must never imitate it or think that it is correct!)

Extension/challenge
Divide the pupils into two equal groups. Take away the name cards from both groups. Take away the noun cards from one group and replace them with plural pronoun cards, such as: *the boys, the girls, the pupils, the students,* etc. Ensure that each pupil has one card, as before. Ask them to quickly find partners from the other group and then take an apostrophe card and place it after the first word to create a clause, such as: *the boys' house* or *the students' classroom.* Remind them that they do not now need an *s* card.

Discuss the particular words that are plurals but follow the singular pattern because they do not end in *s* , such as *children* and *people*. Also discuss the possessive pronouns *his, her* and *its*, which do not need any apostrophes. (The word *it's* only occurs to indicate a missing letter when used to replace two words, such as *it is* – another mistake that many adults make because they didn't learn or understand the rules when they were young!)

What's missing?

Learning objective
Apostrophes to indicate missing letters or words

Preparation
Make a number of cards stating words such as: *did, was, do, should, could, would* and *had*. Make other cards to represent the letters: *n, o* and *t* and apostrophes.

Activity
Give one card to each pupil at random. Ask those with the letters to stand together in threes to create the word *not* several times, while the words and apostrophes wait in separate lines. Ask the pupils with word cards to run, one at a time, and each to stand to the left of a *not* group. As soon as they get there, an apostrophe must run to the *not* group and take the place of the letter *o*, which must run away and sit down on the floor, so that *did not* becomes *didn't*, etc.

Remind pupils that they would only use apostrophes to replace letters, in order to shorten words and make contractions, in informal speech or writing.

Extension/challenge
Try the activity with other words instead of *not*. Sometimes more than one letter is replaced. The apostrophes can replace the *h* and the *a* of *have* (as in *I've*), or the *w* and the *i* of *will* (as in *I'll*), etc.

Talk about irregular word changes to remember and watch out for, such as: *will not* becoming *won't* and *cannot* becoming *can't*.

© Debbie Chalmers and Brilliant Publications

And then ...

Learning objective
Using an ellipsis

Preparation
Find a collection of balls of the same size (roughly one per pupil in the group) and set three of them out in a row. Explain to your pupils that three dots after a word, known as an ellipsis, can be used to indicate that the next words are missing. This may be because they are already known or because the rest is left to the reader's imagination.

A well-known song could be referred to within a text as: *Puff the magic dragon ...* because readers would know the lyrics or could easily find them if needed. A fairy tale might end: *And they rode off into the sunset ...* because that could be the beginning of another story imagined by readers.

Activity
Divide the pupils into groups of four and give each group three balls. Ask them to decide together on a traditional simile, a well-known song, a fantasy story ending and a piece of factual information, then to speak each aloud and follow it with the three dots.
For example:

> *As heavy as ...*
> *Incy Wincy Spider climbed up the water spout ...*
> *He swam away to look for another adventure ...*
> *A lion sleeps all day in the sun, but in the evenings he goes hunting ...*

The groups may perform their ideas to each other, with the four pupils taking turns to speak one of the lines each while the other three members of the group roll the balls into place beside him to create an ellipsis.

Extension/challenge
Invite the pupils to sit in spaces and tell them that you are going to create a story together. Begin by offering them an opening line, such as: *The new teacher had a surprise for his class ...* then break off and say *dot, dot, dot* while pointing to a pupil.

That pupil may stand up and continue the story with one or more sentences from his own imagination, then say *dot, dot, dot* and point to any other seated pupil, who will then do the same thing until everybody has taken a turn and is standing.

The story may be left at the point of the last pupil's *dot, dot, dot*. The chance to take it further might provide a stimulus for creative writing back in the classroom.

Teaching Grammar, Punctuation and Spelling Through Drama

What did he say?

Learning objective
Inverted commas in speech and dialogue

Preparation
Make a collection of cards that read: *he said, she said* and *they said* – several of each. Make other cards that are speeches describing an action, using different tenses, such as: *I'm going to go for a walk, I'm reading my book* and *we carried the heavy shopping*.

Activity
Some pupils can work individually, having one of the cards. Less confident pupils may be asked to work in pairs, having the *they said* cards and the *we …* action cards. Other pairs of pupils represent inverted commas by holding up their arms to form arched shapes that lean over the speeches.

Invite pupils to create sentences by teaming action speeches with *said* cards, then ask the inverted commas to move into the correct spaces and lean in the right directions. Explain that inverted commas are also often called 'speech marks' when used in this way.

Encourage pupils to notice and understand that words enclosed within speech marks are reporting exactly what was said at a particular time, and, therefore, a phrase such as *he said* does not change according to the tense of the speech.

Extension/challenge
Add cards with other phrases that describe speech, such as *he replied, she shouted* or *they asked*, to replace the *said* cards and encourage pupils to use suitable and relevant ones to fit the speeches within their sentences.

Provide action speeches involving questions and answers and challenge pupils to find and match them, then put them together in sentences.

Is that true?

Learning objective

Inverted commas used for effect

Preparation

Create a list of suggestions for words in sentences that may need inverted commas to show that they are implying meaning but not actually true. Explain their use to your pupils, with examples such as:

We met 'Father Christmas' at the garden centre.

The 'horse' was the funniest character in the pantomime.

Her 'birthday cake' was a cucumber with candles in it.

Activity

Invite pupils to work in small groups of five, six or seven. Each group should create their own sentence to speak aloud. Two pupils may form the inverted commas by arching their arms over one pupil who speaks the word(s) to appear inside them. One or two pupils should speak the word(s) that come before them and one or two pupils should speak the word(s) that come after them. They may stand in a line to perform their sentence to everybody else, from left to right, in turn.

Extension/challenge

Invite larger groups to create sentences with more than one word or set of words in inverted commas. The pair of pupils can move to surround each in turn, or groups can include more than one pair of pupils performing as inverted commas.

Teaching Grammar, Punctuation and Spelling Through Drama
© Debbie Chalmers and Brilliant Publications

Make a report

Learning objective
Inverted commas used in exact reporting

Preparation
Gather some microphones to be used as props (toy ones, home-made ones or unconnected ones) and some clipboards with paper and pens.

Activity
Invite pupils to work in pairs and to choose their own topics. One should be a reporter and the other a person who is being interviewed. The reporter should ask a question to obtain facts or an opinion, such as:

> *Why did you go into your garden in the dark?*
> *Do you think children should eat sweets every day?*

He must then write down on his clipboard exactly what the interviewee said in reply.

Ask pairs of pupils then to join up with other pairs, to form groups of four, and to look at each other's clipboards. In turn, the reporters should pretend to speak to a camera and introduce their interviewees. They may talk generally and then report exactly what was said. As each reporter speaks, the other pair, who are now the inverted commas, need to listen carefully and be ready to hold up their hands to indicate the beginning and end of the speech made by the interviewee. If desired, the interviewee can speak again to add further facts or opinions after the inverted commas.

Extension/challenge
Repeat the activity with no interviews. Each pupil in turn may pretend to be a television or radio newsreader reporting on the day's events. Two other pupils should guess where the exact reported speech comes and hold up their hands as before. If they need a clue, encourage them to listen out for phrases which include speech words, such as: *the girl smiled as she replied* or *they shouted excitedly.*

It can be tricky to be sure of exactly where a speech begins or ends when hearing it for the first time, so you may choose to allow each group to practise once and then to repeat the activity correctly in performance to each other.

What happened next?

Learning objective
Dashes

Preparation
Explain to your pupils that a dash can be used between words, clauses or phrases within a sentence, to hold them apart. It is stronger than a comma, but not so strong as a full stop. With experience, pupils will learn to be more confident about when to use a comma, a semi-colon or a dash. Suggest to them that they listen in their heads to sentences as they write them and try using a dash if they are hoping to create a 'cliffhanger moment' before offering an answer, a clarification, an explanation, an opinion, an emphasis or an opposite.

Make up a list of statements that you can say to pupils to encourage them to give answers that might follow a dash.

Activity
Divide the pupils into six groups. Explain that, when it is his turn, you would like a pupil to lie down on the floor in a stretched thin shape to indicate a dash and then to stand up and speak the word or words that will follow the dash.

Offer a statement to the first group that requires an answer after a dash, such as:
> *I bought my favourite vegetable yesterday – carrots.*

As you repeat the statement for each pupil in the group in turn, ask him to mime the dash and then offer a different idea (*beetroot, onions, spinach,* etc).

Repeat the activity with the second group, asking for a clarification, such as:

> *Make sure you've done your work first – the maths problems.*

The third group can be asked for an explanation, using a statement such as:
> *You mustn't go onto the grass today – it's too wet and muddy.*

The fourth group may offer an opinion, such as:
> *The first team played hockey – they weren't as good as last year's team.*

Invite the fifth group to add emphasis after their dashes. For example:
> *We must leave in time – we can't be late!*

The sixth group can use a dash to balance opposites, as in:
> *I like to watch films on television – my sister likes cartoons.*

Extension/challenge
Ask the pupils to form groups of three and to create their own sentences containing dashes. They may then demonstrate them to everybody else, in turn.

One pupil should speak the first part of the sentence, which will be the statement, one should form the dash by lying down in a thin shape between the other two, and the third should speak the words that form an answer, a clarification, an explanation, an opinion, an emphasis or an opposite. Encourage each group to identify which type of sentence they have made, supporting them if necessary, and find out which is the easiest or most popular type of sentence to create when including a dash.

And also ...

Learning objective
Brackets to enclose extra information

Preparation
Make word cards that can be put together to form simple comparative or descriptive sentences, such as:

> *The new green grass was softer than the old brown grass.*

Some words that would always maintain their order, such as *was softer than*, may appear together on one card, to be held by one pupil, if the group is small.

Activity
Give each card to one pupil and invite the group of pupils with cards to discuss the words together and shuffle around until they form a sentence. Ask other pupils to work in pairs to represent brackets. They can decide which words within a sentence should be enclosed within brackets, then stand at each side of them and reach out their arms towards each other, to enclose them.

There may be more than one set of brackets within a sentence and more than one choice for the brackets. For example: *The new (green) grass … or The (new) green grass….*

Extension/challenge
Make the sentences more complex, to include more than one word inside the brackets. For example:

> *The cars drove quickly along the motorway (which had been re-surfaced the week before), finding it much quieter and smoother.*

And by the way ...

Learning objective
Brackets to add an aside

Preparation
Make cards to represent phrases that can be put together to form sentences. Include objects, subjects, verbs and adjectives. Also include some phrases that could appear in brackets as asides. For example:

> *The tallest girl (who had long hair) always wore a hat when she used the lawn mower (that belonged to her father) to cut the grass.*

Activity
Give each card to one pupil, asking the others to wait to represent pairs of brackets. Encourage the pupils to discuss ideas with each other and to shuffle around and change places until they are standing in order, in a line from left to right, to create a sentence that makes sense.

Invite pairs of pupils to discuss where the brackets should go and then to jump into the line and reach out their arms towards each other, to enclose the phrases that should be contained within brackets.

Extension/challenge
Make some phrases on cards that could fit many different situations, such as:

> *(very quietly)*
> *(who was very tired)*
> *(after the party)*

Ask some pupils to form groups of three – one to hold the phrase and two to be the brackets enclosing it.

Invite other pupils to make up beginnings of sentences, involving a subject with or without an action, and to say them aloud. For example:

> *The three boys*
> *The dog went home*
> *The tiny baby*
> *The woman was sad*

Invite the rest of the pupils to make up endings for the sentences, involving a verb and an adjective, and to say them aloud. For example:

> *ran home quickly*
> *slept for a long time*
> *and went to bed*

Encourage pupils to move around, trying out different bracketed asides in different sentences and matching beginnings with endings around them, until they form sensible sentences. They will need to speak the sentences aloud to hear and check whether the words flow correctly. (Connecting words such as *who, was* or *and* are needed after an action, but are not used immediately after a subject.) All parts of the sentences must be in the same tense.

The past tense is usually the easiest for pupils to hear and check; if they become practised at the activity, move on to try using the present tense.

Teaching Grammar, Punctuation and Spelling Through Drama

I'll tell you more

Learning objective
Brackets to give further explanation

Preparation
Make a list of places and situations in which people might find themselves or things might happen, such as: on a building site, up a mountain, on a beach, in a wood, at a wedding, at a relative's house for tea and at a birthday party.

Activity
Give each pair or small group of pupils a place or situation. Ask them each to think of a relevant sentence that they can say and act out. For example:

We always put on our hard hats and strong boots when we work on the building site.

Ask each pair or group, in turn, to perform their sentence and ask everybody to listen carefully to all the sentences, as they will need to think of ideas to add to them.

As each pair or group then performs their sentence again, invite any other pupil to think of and suggest an explanation that could be added to it, in brackets. For example:

(because we might hit our heads)
(to keep us safe from falling bricks)

The first pupil to offer a relevant explanation may choose two others to stand at either side of him, as brackets, and take them with him to fit the explanation into the sentence. The original pair or group must allow them in and then they can all say the new sentence, speaking in turn. The brackets may come at the end or somewhere in the middle (which is why there must be at least two pupils to say the original sentence, so that they may retain and speak their own phrases if they are split apart by the bracketed phrase.)

Extension/challenge
Ask pupils to attempt to fit two explanations within brackets into one sentence. For example:

I went for a wintry walk (on the coldest day of last year), slipped on the ice and broke my arm (in two places).

Or challenge them to create a group of sentences all related to one situation, each with an explanation within brackets. For example:

You can put any vegetables together to make soup (and it's a good way of using up leftovers). Add some potatoes (because they give it a thicker texture). Don't use onions and leeks (since they taste too similar). Carrots are good because of their bright colour, but chop them into very small pieces (or they won't be soft enough when the rest of the vegetables are ready). Be adventurous with flavours and add seasonings and spices if you like them, but not too much pepper (or your soup will make you sneeze)!

On the other hand

Learning objective

Semi-colons to separate or balance contradictions

Preparation

Create some examples of sentences presenting contradictions and read and discuss them with your pupils before beginning the activity, to ensure that they understand what they will be working to achieve. For example:

Cats are smaller and chase mice; dogs are bigger and chase cats.

Evergreen trees keep their leaves all year round; deciduous trees lose their leaves in autumn.

Activity

Divide the pupils into an even number of pairs or small groups and ask some pupils to represent semi-colons by holding up a fist above a bent forearm. One semi-colon is needed for each two groups. Ask each group to create half a sentence involving three ideas, such as: an animal, its size and its food, or a vehicle, its speed and its destination. Give each set of three ideas to two groups who will work independently and it is most likely that they will choose differently and therefore create a contradictory sentence.

Invite each two pairs or groups in turn to say their sentence and ask a semi-colon to jump into the middle and stand between them. Suggest to the pupils that a semi-colon may often be used in place of a connecting word, such as *but, while* or *however*. The two phrases

that it connects may often work as short stand-alone sentences, but, when connected, they make longer and more varied sentences and contribute to more interesting and mature writing.

Extension/challenge

Provide some scales with weights to balance them and demonstrate how one side may tip down until balanced by the other and how making the two sides equally heavy keeps them level.

Invite pupils to say their sentences again, this time moving gradually down to squatting or kneeling as they speak, then gradually standing up again to be level with each other once the semi-colon has jumped into place.

I don't think so

Learning objective

Semi-colons to separate or balance preferences or opinions

Preparation

Talk with your pupils about preferences and opinions, explaining that everybody has preferences and is entitled to their own opinions, but that we should always try to respect each other as much as possible.

Activity

Invite each pupil to choose a partner, or choose the pairs yourself to allow those of similar ability levels to work together. Give each pair a subject that they could safely disagree on, such as favourite colours, foods or types of music, what to do at weekends or where to go on holiday. Ask them to create an argument! (They are likely to find it hard to believe that they are being encouraged to do this and relish the challenge!) Stress that it must be conducted within a dialogue in which each has a fair chance to speak, that it must be polite verbal disagreement only and that it is acting (ie not really feeling annoyed with each other)!

Ask them to end the argument by agreeing to differ and creating a summarizing sentence to say together, such as:

I like red; I prefer green.
I go out for walks and to play at the park; I stay at home and read or draw.

As they speak, they can form a semi-colon between them, if one pupil holds out a fist and the other holds out a bent forearm below it. Suggest that the semi-colon is taking the place of a connecting word such as *but* or *although*.

Extension/challenge

Ask pupils to prepare their speeches to perform to the rest of the group in character, pretending to be two younger children or older people, storybook characters or talking animals. Encourage character voices and original ideas.

Ask for the summarizing sentence, with the semi-colon, at the end of each speech.

Is there a reason?

Learning objective

Semi-colons to separate or balance explanations or comparisons

Preparation

Talk with your pupils about sentences that offer explanations for events or people's feelings, such as:

Not many people came to the fête; it rained all day and the field was very muddy.
They didn't enjoy their walk; it was very cold and windy.

Discuss how sentences can contain comparisons (in any tense), such as:

Last winter was very cold; this winter has been warmer.
The maths exam is very difficult; the history exam is easier.
Going to work in the morning will be simple enough; coming back in the dark will be harder.

Activity

Divide the pupils into three equal groups. Ask each pupil in the first group to make up the first half of a sentence, describing something that happened or how somebody felt. Ask each pupil in the second group to make up the second half of a sentence, giving a description or an explanation. Ask the pupils in the third group to represent semi-colons by holding out a fist above a bent forearm.

Invite the pupils of the first group, in turn, to stand up and speak their phrases aloud. After each one, ask a semi-colon to stand beside him and then ask the second group for a volunteer to complete the sentence by standing beside the semi-colon and speaking his phrase aloud. These pupils must listen carefully and think about which phrases might be good matches for theirs, as the two parts need to be at least vaguely relevant and must make sense. (Remind them that their phrases must not begin with *because*, as the semi-colon is the connective.)

Ask the three groups to swap roles and repeat the activity, then swap again and repeat it again, until each pupil has taken a turn in each role. (This could happen within one session or spread over two or three consecutive sessions.)

Extension/challenge

Once all of the pupils have fully grasped the concept of using semi-colons correctly within sentences that contain relevant explanations or comparisons, allow them to have fun by putting together irrelevant ones, so that they can see that both words and punctuation are important and must work together. For example, they may create crazy sentences, such as:

Dogs don't like carrots; flowers go to sleep when it snows.
Camels dance in the deserts; people eat woolly hats in winter.

For crazy sentence ideas and to develop pupils' confidence in using more varied vocabulary, provide access to a selection of books by Dr Seuss and collections of nonsense poems by various authors.

A whole group

Learning objective
Colons before lists

Preparation
Write some phrases on paper or card that introduce lists, such as:

> *In a zoo, the animals are:*
> *In a rainbow, the colours are:*

Stick them on the walls around the room.

Activity
Secretly tell each pupil the word that they will represent, such as: *red, yellow, blue, tigers, camels, penguins, cars, lorries, buses, trees, flowers* or *grass.*

Ask the pupils to walk around the room, reading all the signs and deciding which one they should stop at. When all of the pupils have chosen, go to each group in turn and read out the phrase. Each pupil should then take his cue and say his word to check whether he is in the right list. For example, you should hear:

> *In a zoo, the animals are: tigers, camels, penguins, monkeys, lions, elephants* (or something similar).

If a pupil finds that he is in the wrong list (eg tiger in the rainbow or blue in a zoo), ask the other pupils to help him to find the right group to move into.

Show the pupils how to represent a colon using two fists held out one above the other, then divide them into groups of five to eight members. Invite each group to create their own list, with one pupil offering the opening phrase, one making the colon and the other three to six pupils naming relevant items, one after the other.

Extension/challenge
Remind pupils that, when they are writing a list, each item will be followed by a comma, that the word *and* will appear between the last two items and that there will be a full stop at the end of the list. Explain that the words may all be spoken, the colon may be represented by two fists, commas may crawl into place and the full stop may jump.

Ask the groups to join together in pairs, or make new groups with at least ten members in each. Invite them to create new sentences including an opening phrase, a colon and items separated by commas and the word *and*, with a full stop at the end.

Your turn

Learning objective

Colons before speeches or instructions

Preparation

Read some plays or dialogues with your pupils before attempting this activity and draw their attention to the way they are laid out, with a character's name followed by a colon before each speech.

Ask each pupil to make his own name on a card and invite some to write down some questions and answers on longer pieces of card.

Activity

Divide the pupils into three equal groups. Ask one group to hold up their names, one group to represent colons by holding out two fists, one above the other, and one group to hold up questions and answers (that match each other). Encourage pupils to move around, discussing ideas and helping each other, and to organize themselves into a simple script or dialogue in which a colon stands beside a name and a question beside the colon, facing another name, another colon and an answer. They may then speak the dialogue aloud, either individually or in unison.

In this way, a class of thirty pupils would create five questions and five answers with ten names and ten colons. Invite them to swap cards with each other and reform the dialogues with different pupils representing names, colons, questions and answers.

Extension/challenge

Explain that instructions for different people may be written down in the same way. Instead of questions and answers, use movement words. Each pupil representing a name or a colon then makes the movement that is on the card of the person standing beside him. For example, he may dance, jump, hop, jog, spin, sway or shake. Ask pupils to change places with each other at least twice, so that they all take turns to make the movements.

Begin to rhyme

Learning objective
Initial letters and rhymes

Preparation
Read books of rhymes and poetry with your pupils and explore stories told in rhyme. Chant and sing rhymes and songs together. Discuss how it is often possible to work out the spelling of a word by thinking of a rhyming word that you already know and using phonetic knowledge to change the beginning while keeping the rest of the spelling pattern.

Activity
Invite the pupils each to represent a different letter of the alphabet. Ask them to write the letters clearly on large stickers and attach them to their clothing. Think of some common spelling patterns together, such as: *at, un, ing, ent, eam, ough* and *ould*.

Ask the pupils representing the appropriate letters to stand in lines (reading from left to right), to form one or more of the word endings. Invite the other pupils to move to stand at the beginnings of lines if they can form words. When an initial letter joins with the others in a line, all of the pupils may act out the word.

For example: *c* walks to *at* and the three pupils pretend to be *cats; s* walks to *ing* and the four pupils begin to *sing; t* walks to *ough* and the five pupils mime the word *tough*, perhaps by holding up fists to show strength and muscles or by pretending to push or pull something that is heavy or stuck.

If there are fewer than 26 pupils in the group, leave out some of the less used letters, such as *q, x* and *z*. If you need double or frequently occurring letters, such as *e, a, o, l, t* and *s*, allow more than one pupil to represent the same letter. A pupil could even have one letter on his front and a different one on his back!

Repeat the activity using two or three letter blends to begin the words, such as: *ch, th, tr, sm, thr* or *scr*, but keeping the endings. Up to seven letters may then stand in line together to form a word and it is quite likely that a letter may need to appear more than once. Invite the pupils to act out their words again. For example: *chat, thing, through* or *scream*.

Extension/challenge
Remind the pupils that not all rhyming words are spelt similarly and not all words with the same spelling patterns are pronounced in the same way. Divide them into small groups and give each group a different rhyming word to act out. For example: *good, hood, wood, would, could* and *should*. Then give each group a word using the same spelling pattern, many of which may sound different. For example: t*ough, rough, enough, cough, bough* and *through*. Invite them to act out the words in turn for the other groups to identify.

Make a pattern

Learning objective

Common spelling patterns

Preparation

Make available a selection of simple books that your pupils read when they were younger. Use books from the school reading scheme and picture book stories, especially those told in rhyme. Allow the pupils enough time to read them independently, as they are bound to enjoy having an excuse to explore old favourites. (Tell them that they are using the books for research!)

Invite pupils to work in small groups to find and make lists of common spelling patterns that appear in many words. Then ask the groups to share and discuss their lists and work with them to create one combined list that includes everybody's ideas.

Ask the pupils to write each letter that appears in a spelling pattern onto a square card and to choose one each to hold up. (If the group is small, they could choose two each; if it is large, they could include more than one of the most common letters.) If some of the patterns have duplicated letters, such as *all* or *ness*, include them. While they do this, make other squares representing letters and blends that often begin words, such as: *b, c, h, m, p, s, t, ch, th, scr* and *thr*.

Activity

Hold up different letters in turn as initial sounds and ask pupils to run to stand in a line to make a word, with letters reading from left to right. For example: hold up *c* and the four pupils with *o, u, g, h*, or the four pupils with *a, t, c, h*, or the five pupils with *a, u, g, h, t* could make words. Choose a very different initial sound next, such as *scr*, so that other pupils can make words like *scream, scratch* and *script*.

Encourage them to discuss their letters and words, to work together and to make several different words, one after the other, calling out each word aloud to ensure that everybody in the group understands.

Extension/challenge

Give the initial letters and blends to various pupils and ask them to move amongst the group, choosing a set of letters to join them in a line to make a word.

Swap several times, so that all pupils have opportunities to work both as an initial letter or blend and as a word letter.

Spells of wizardry

Learning objective
'Magic e' words

Preparation
Talk with your pupils about the phonetic sounds and the names of letters, especially the five vowels, and check that they all understand them clearly. Remind them that a 'magic e' added to the end of a word can change its pronunciation and meaning because the vowel will now use its name instead of its sound and the 'magic e' is silent. (This works for *a, i, o* and *u*, but not for *e* itself.)

Ask them each to write a large letter *e* onto a square card and attach it to a stick, straw or pipe cleaner, to be used as a magic wand. Also make lots of other letters on cards, that can form words to be changed by a 'magic e'. You will need several of each of the vowels *a, i, o* and *u* and lots of consonants. (Think of the words in your head as you make the appropriate letters for them, as so many three letter words are actually irregular.)

Also, provide thin black or coloured card, shirring or cord elastic, paper stars or stickers, glue, sticky tape, pens and scissors and invite all pupils to make wizards' hats and cloaks.

Activity
Choose a quarter of the group to be wizards first and invite them to dress up and have their magic wands ready. Give each of the other pupils a letter. Ask them to form threes to create 'consonant, vowel, consonant' (cvc) words and to mime or act them out together. For example: *mad, fir, hop* or *cut*. Then ask the wizards to bring their 'magic e' wands to change the words and invite the four pupils now in each line to mime or act out the new word. For example: *made, fire, hope* or *cute*.

Repeat the activity three times, in one session or in consecutive sessions, to allow all pupils to take turns to be wizards.

Extension/challenge
Introduce sound blends to begin words, instead of single letters, and repeat the activity to form and change words. For example: *spar* to *spare*, *twin* to *twine*, *slop* to *slope* or *plum* to *plume*.

The miming or acting out of some of the words could become quite challenging, but encourage pupils to use their imaginations and ingenuity and 'have a go'. You may need to help by explaining the meanings of some words verbally.

Already happened

Learning objective
Adding 'ed' to regular words to make the past tense

Preparation
Make word cards representing regular verbs in the present tense, that just take *ed* in the past tense, such as: *look, climb* and *wait*. (Avoid those that end in *e*, those that need a doubled consonant and those that have irregular past participles.) Also make lots of square cards to represent the letter *e* and the letter *d*.

Activity
Divide the pupils into three groups. Give the first group each a letter *e* and the second group each a letter *d*. Give the third group each a word and invite them to walk around, miming their words. Ask the pupils representing the two different letters to form pairs (to make *ed*) and to set out together to choose a word and to join in with its mime. (The mime would not look significantly different just because the verb has changed from the present to the past tense.)

Extension/challenge
Discuss with pupils the verbs that have irregular past participles and do not use *ed* at all. Challenge them to think of and say as many as they can. For example: *ran, sang, sat, fell, saw, ate* and *bought*. Make favourite story and poetry books available if pupils need to use them to discover and check words.

Sit with the pupils in a group or a circle and invite them to take turns to mime one of the words for everybody to guess.

Teaching Grammar, Punctuation and Spelling Through Drama
© Debbie Chalmers and Brilliant Publications

Scare him off

Learning objective

Adding 'ed' to words ending in 'e'

Preparation

Make word cards representing verbs that end in *e* in the present tense, such as: *dance, squeeze, skate* and *smile*. Miss off the final letter *e* when writing each word. Also make the same number of separate square cards representing the letter *d* and twice as many representing the letter *e*.

Activity

Divide the pupils into four groups. One group will each have a different word (without the final *e*), one group will each have a letter *d* and two groups will each have a letter *e*. Ask each pupil representing a word to join with one of the pupils representing a letter *e* and encourage them to walk around miming the word together. Invite the rest of the pupils representing letter *e* and all of the pupils representing letter *d* to form pairs and then to join with the words. As an *ed* pair joins a word, they may pretend to be scary and the *e* that is already there must pretend to be afraid and run away.

Extension/challenge

Introduce verbs that end in the letter *y*, such as: *carry, hurry* and *worry*. You will need to miss off the letter *y* from the word cards and make separate *y* cards. Also make cards to represent the letter *i* and use the *e* and *d* cards as before.

Divide the pupils into five groups. Invite each pupil representing a word to join with one representing a letter *y* and ask them to walk around miming the word together, as before. Ask those representing the letters *e* and *d* to form pairs again and choose to join with words, while those representing the letter *i* watch and wait. As an *ed* pair joins a word, an *i* should run between them and the *y* should pretend to be scared and run away.

Double time

Learning objective
Adding 'ed' and doubling consonants

Preparation
Make word cards representing verbs that end in a consonant in the present tense, which is doubled when the past tense is formed by the addition of *ed*. For example: *beg, pat, stir* and *stop*. Make lots of square cards with the letter *e* and with the letter *d* on them. Also make squares with the individual consonants needed. (These will probably be: *b, d, g, l, n, p, r* and *t*.)

Activity
Divide the pupils into four seated groups. Give each member of the first group a word, each of the second group a letter *e*, each of the third group a letter *d* and each of the fourth group a separate consonant. Invite the first group to stand up in turn to mime their words. While a word is being mimed, a letter *e* should move from his group to choose a letter *d*. The pair should then, together, go to join with a word, while the single consonants watch carefully. As soon as the *ed* pair reaches the word, the correct consonant may jump up and walk between them, so doubling the final consonant and linking the word with its ending.

To make the game more exciting, the word with the consonant and the *ed* pair could pretend to be two-headed monsters who try to scare each other before deciding to unite and be friends!

Play the game on several occasions, so that all pupils may take turns to explore each of the different roles.

Extension/challenge
Invite the pupils to work as a group to write individual letters of the alphabet on squares of card. They should aim to make at least four of each letter. (It won't matter if they're not all used after all.) Spread out the letters around the room, in 26 piles on the floor.

Invite two pupils at a time to secretly think of a verb in its past tense, then to run to collect the letters they need, arrange them in order on the floor for the group to see and perform appropriate mimes to illustrate them. (It's unlikely that they will independently choose the same word as each other, but, if it happens, it's just amusing.) Explain to pupils that when a verb has a double letter in the present (eg *call*), it only needs the addition of *ed* to form the past tense.

Decide as a whole group whether the words are spelt correctly. If there is a mistake, another pupil may volunteer to correct it by swapping letters around, while everybody else calls out ideas and clues to help them. Especially praise those pupils who choose more complicated or difficult verbs to try, even if they are unsure that their spelling will be correct, rather than 'playing safe' and sticking only to the simple and often more boring ones.

Do it now

Learning objective

Adding 'ing' to regular verbs in the present tense

Preparation

Make word cards representing regular verbs in the present tense, that take *ing* without losing or doubling their last letters, such as: *crawl, sleep* and *whisper*. Also make a number of cards representing: *I, we, am, are* and *ing*. For a class of 30 pupils, make:

> *I* x 4
> *we* x 6
> *am* x 2
> *are* x 3
> *ing* x five
> two copies of each of five verbs

Explain to the pupils that there are two forms of the present tense in the English language. For example: *I sing* and *I am singing*. The first form is often used to describe something that happens frequently, or something that is occurring now but will end soon. The second form is usually used to indicate something that is going on now and may last a while. It is only with practice that pupils will learn to hear and decide which of the two to use in various situations, but their spellings may be learned quite easily.

Activity

Give one card to each pupil. Ask them all to move around the room looking for others to join with to make phrases. Some will form pairs, as in: *I walk* or *we roll*. Others will make groups of four, as in: *I am falling* or *we are jumping*.

Invite the pairs and the groups of four to stand on two separate 'islands' – one in each half of the room. Invite all of the pupils to practise performing their actions. If they are a pair or a group containing *I*, they should perform one after the other (as *I* means one person). If they are a pair or a group containing *we*, they should perform together (as *we* means more than one person).

Ask one pair to begin, with their one or two performances of their action. The group of four with the corresponding action should then take their cue and give their one or four performances. Choose another pair to take the next turn and continue in this way until all pupils have performed. (It's a good idea to ask pupils to sit down after completing their turn, so that it's easy to tell who is still to perform.)

Extension/challenge

Invite the pupils to form new groups of four and to decide on an action together, then take turns to perform it for everybody else to guess. Each time the group guesses correctly, they may all chant the phrase together (and stand up and copy the action if they like). For example: *We are flying!*

Swap with me

Learning objective

Adding 'ing' to words ending in 'e'

Preparation

Make word cards representing verbs that end in *e* in the present tense, such as: *pounce, stride* and *freeze*, but omit the letter *e* from the word cards and write them on separate squares of card instead. Also, make an equal number of cards to represent *ing*.

Activity

Divide the pupils into three groups. Give the first group each a word card, the second group each an *e* card and the third group each an *ing* card. Ask the words to stand in spaces and those with *e* and *ing* cards to stand in groups to wait.

When you call 'Go!', the *e* cards may go quickly to the words and form pairs, then all perform their actions simultaneously until you call 'Stop!' They then freeze until you call 'Go!' again, when the *ing* cards go quickly to swap places with the *e* cards and join the words in performing the actions again. Repeat the 'Stop!' and 'Go!' calls as many times as you like. The *e* and *ing* cards take alternate turns with each other, but they may go to a different word each time it is their turn. Allow the pupils to swap roles, until they have each had a turn to be a word, an *e* and an *ing*.

Extension/challenge

Challenge the pupils to think of longer and more complicated words that they can add *ing* to, such as: *remember, imagine, develop, capsize, photograph* and *impersonate*. Ask them to write the words onto cards and to discuss and decide together whether they need to lose an *e* before adding an *ing*. Encourage half of the group to take a word each and the other half to use the *ing* cards. Invite them all to form pairs and to fold away the final *e* behind the rest of the word when the *ing* joins it, if necessary.

Sensitively offer help with the spelling of some of the longer words if pupils become confused or make a mistake that they cannot see or correct. They should be encouraged to try to use new and adventurous words and to add them to the vocabulary of the group. The aim is to learn to spell and remember a variety of words by the end of the activity, but not right from the beginning.

It takes two

Learning objective

Adding 'ing' and doubling consonants

Preparation

Make word cards representing verbs that double their final consonants when *ing* is added to them. For example: *drag, clap* and *sit*. Also, make lots of cards with *ing* on them and square cards representing the individual consonants that may be doubled (*b, d, g, l, n, p, r* and *t*).

Activity

Divide the pupils into three groups. Give a word card to each pupil in the first group. Give a single consonant card to each pupil in the second group and an *ing* card to each pupil in the third group. Ask the pupils of the second group to stand in spaces, while the third group, with *ing* cards, wait in a line.

Invite the first group to walk around, looking at all the cards, until they find the right letters to match the consonants at the ends of their words. As they find them, they may bow to the letters and invite them to join them.

The pairs should then walk together to the third group, where they each bow to one pupil and invite the *ing* to join their word. Each group of three may then act out their own action together.

Extension/challenge

Invite pupils to work in small groups (of three to six members). Offer a theme and ask each group to think of and mime a related word ending in *ing* for everybody else to guess. For example, on the theme of speech: *whispering, talking, shouting, calling, grumbling*, etc. If two groups choose the same word, praise both and then challenge them both to think of different ones.

Repeat the activity with as many themes as you like, such as: moving along the floor (*crawling, sliding, rolling, shuffling, squirming*), or moving quickly (*running, skipping, hopping, spinning, wriggling*).

After each theme, ask each group to state whether their word was regular, or lost an *e*, or doubled a consonant. If they are not sure, ask the other groups to help them to decide.

More of us

Learning objective

Regular plurals – adding 's' or 'es'

Preparation

Make two lists of words – one of nouns that take *s* to form their plurals and one of nouns that take *es* to form their plurals. The two lists should consist of sets of words that are linked or follow a theme. For example:

cucumber	*tomato*
skirt	*dress*
king	*princess*
carrot	*potato*
wizard	*witch*
farm	*beach*
comb	*brush*

Write the words onto separate cards. Also make square cards to represent the letter *e* and twice as many to represent the letter *s*.

Activity

Give one card to each pupil. Invite those with a letter *e* to form pairs with half of those with a letter *s*. Then, ask each pupil with a word, in turn, to choose whether to stand beside a single letter *s* or a pair of pupils representing *es*.

When all of the words have been made plural in this way, ask the letters if they think that all of the words are correct. If not, allow them to swap with other letters. Encourage the group to call out to help each other and work together to make all of the words right.

Invite pupils to decide which of the words go together and to create groups of five by linking each pair with the relevant trio and standing together (eg *cucumbers* and *tomatoes*).

Extension/challenge

Ask pupils to look carefully at the words that take *es* and to identify the letters that they usually end with (*h, o, ss* and *x*).

Encourage them to think of words that end in *e*, such as: *cake, house* or *sausage*, and to write them on cards and add *s* cards to them, in order to understand that adding an *s* to these words should not be confused with adding *es* to others.

Yes, I'm coming

Learning objectives
Irregular plurals – words ending in 'y'

Preparation
Invite your pupils to help to think of words that end in the letter *y* and create a list together. The words may be a mixture of nouns, such as: *curry, jelly* or *dolly*, and verbs, such as: *carry, hurry* or *bury*. Write the beginnings of the words (without the letter *y*) onto cards and make an equal number of square cards to represent the letters *y, i* and *es*.

Activity
Give one card to each pupil. Invite each word to join with a letter *y* and ask the pairs to stand in spaces in one half of the room, while those with the *i* and *es* cards stand in groups in the other half of the room.

Teach the pupils the following dialogue (reminding them that they are just acting when they shout at each other!).

Word (*shouts to letter* y):   Go away!
The letter *y* (*shouts*):   Why?
The letter *i* (*shouts*):   I am coming!
(*The letter* i *then runs to replace the letter* y, *who runs away and stands beside the* es *instead.*)
The *es* (*shouts*):   Yes!
(*The* y *then runs away and sits down and the* es *runs to stand beside the* i *to form the plural of the word.*)

Each group then acts out their word. For example:

curry	miming eating a hot curry
jelly	wobbling like a jelly
dolly	holding and rocking a dolly
carry	carrying something heavy
hurry	hurrying around in a circle
bury	digging a hole to bury an item

Play the game at different times, allowing the pupils to take turns in each role. Once they understand how the letters speak their names (eg *y* shouts '*Why*') and form new words, they become stimulated and excited by this activity.

Extension/challenge
Challenge pupils to think of words that end in *ey* and explain that they are irregular and don't follow a pattern. Ask who can describe what one of the words does. For example: *monkey* and *key* just take an *s* for their plurals, while *money* works as a plural word with no additions. Invite each pupil who gives a correct description to go on to act out the word.

Change the letter

Learning objective
Irregular plurals – words ending in 'f'

Preparation
Think of words that end in *f* and take *ves* as plurals. For example: *hoof, half, leaf* and *belief.* Write the beginnings of the words (without the *f*) onto cards and also make the same number of cards to represent *es*.

Activity
Divide the pupils into four groups. Give the word cards to the first group and invite them to stand in spaces. Give the *es* cards to the second group and ask them to wait. Demonstrate for the third group how to turn yourself into a letter *f*, by standing sideways, holding your arms up above your head and bending the hands downwards to form the arched top. Demonstrate for the fourth group how to turn yourself into a letter *v*, by holding your arms and hands straight and pushing them upwards with your elbows touching.

Ask each letter *f* to go to join a word and stand beside it, then each *es* to go to stand beside an *f*. As soon as they get there, encourage the letter *v* to crawl into position in front of an *f* and to gradually stand up to replace it in the lines. Once it is hidden behind a *v*, the *f* pretends to vanish and moves away to sit down.

Extension/challenge
Encourage pupils to think of similar words that are exceptions to the rules when becoming plural and to act them out.

For words such as *roof* or *dwarf*, they should refuse all other letters and accept only an *s* (which could be formed by a pupil making a curved shape with knees and arms while standing).

For words such as *knife*, they should push away the *f* and the *e* before accepting a *v* and an *es*.

They may also think of a word, such as *groove*, which never has an *f*, but appears the same as the words that end in *f* once it accepts an *s* to become plural.

Teaching Grammar, Punctuation and Spelling Through Drama

Leave me alone

Learning objective
Irregular plurals – words that stay the same

Preparation
Make up a list of words that stay the same whether singular or plural, such as: *sheep, grass, money* and *trousers*.

Activity
Suggest one of the words to each pupil and ask them to mime or act out their words in turn. Choose the words carefully to provide an appropriate level of challenge for each pupil. Some words, such as *sheep*, are simple to act out, while others, such as *money*, can easily be indicated symbolically. You may allow a pupil to point or sign to indicate a word such as *trousers*, or he may choose to create a mime involving putting on a pair. But, a word like *grass* could be interesting to mime and might demand some original thinking and ingenuity!

Extension/challenge
Divide the pupils into two equal groups and ask each group in turn to pretend to be the letter *s*, while the pupils of the other group continue to act out their words.

A letter *s* may try to stand beside a word, but every time they will be pushed (very gently) away.

They may try to distract the actors by making funny faces or movements, and, as each actor laughs or stops acting, he must sit down.

Mix up

Learning objective
Unusual plurals

Preparation
Think of words that have unusual plurals – changing *ou* for *i* , *s* for *c*, *ee* for *oo*, *us* for *i*, or adding *en*, etc. Make a list of examples, such as: *mouse/mice, goose/geese, cactus/cacti* and *ox/oxen.*

Activity
Ask the pupils to sit in two equal groups, facing each other. Encourage each group to think and talk together about words that change completely in the plural, and to write a list, keeping it a secret from the other group. When they have at least three or four words each, invite them to take turns to call out a word so that the other group can name the plural. (You may wish to check the two lists before they begin the game to remove any duplicates and suggest alternatives.)

Each time a plural is guessed correctly, the guessers act out the word. If a plural cannot be guessed, those posing the question act out the word and then give the answer.

Extension/challenge
Invite pupils to make the letters of the alphabet on separate stickers that they may wear on the front of their clothing. Include several of each of the vowels and the more popular consonants. Choose pupils to create words by each representing a letter and standing in lines for the letters to be read from left to right. They should call out their letters in turn and then speak the word in unison before miming it.

Ask other pupils, representing different letters, to change the words to their plurals by swapping with those in the lines, calling out the names of their letters as they run, so that those in line can predict what is about to happen.

For example: Six pupils representing the word *cactus* stand in a line, but, when a letter *i* runs to the line, the *u* and the *s* run away. Five pupils representing *mouse* stand in a line, but, when *i* and *c* run to the line, *o, u* and *s* run away.

The new letters must stand in the lines correctly to replace the original ones. The pupils may then call out their letters in turn again, speak the new word in unison and mime it together.

End it now

Learning objective
Word endings – that sound the same and are often confused

Preparation
Make cards to represent common word endings, such as: *ant, ent, ure, our, ory, ary, ery, or, er* and *re*. Think of words that have these endings and make more cards to represent the beginnings of words that will fit with the endings. For example:

> relev/ant
> governm/ent
> pict/ure
> col/our
> obligat/ory
> diction/ary
> arch/ery
> doct/or
> build/er
> theat/re

Don't make them all simple words!

Activity
Give one card to each pupil and ask them all to help each other to decide on and form pairs that will create sensible, real words. All of the pupils must be in appropriate pairs to complete the activity, so, if different words are made and any pupils are left without partners, the group must decide who should swap and how they could reshuffle.

Finally, ask each pair to explain what their word means, verbally and by acting it out. If they don't know, ask other pupils to help them out, and, if nobody knows, explain it yourself.

Extension/challenge
Introduce some identical sounding words with different meanings, such as: *stationary / stationery* and *currant / current*.

Divide the group of pupils into two halves and ask the first group to act out one of the words and the second group to act out the other. Call one the *a* group and one the *e* group (or something relevant), so that pupils will be able to picture the actors in the groups as an aid to memory when writing the words in the future.

How does it end?

Learning objective
Word endings – that can be hard to remember

Preparation
Write the word endings: *able, ous, y* and *ily* clearly onto cards and stick them up onto the walls or at the corners. Also make some cards representing words that end in the letter *e*, but omit the last letter and make separate cards for the letter *e*. Include nouns, such as: *noise, ice, shade, breeze, stone, juice* and *snake*, as well as verbs, such as: *change, shake, wobble, notice, manage, imagine* and *believe*.

Activity
Give one word card to each pupil (or pair of pupils if the group is large). Put the letter *e* cards into a pile in the middle of the hall or room. Ask each pupil to decide on the best ending for his word and then to think about whether he needs to collect an *e* card to make the word, or whether his word drops its *e* to add the ending.

When all of the pupils are ready, they should walk quickly to stand beside their chosen ending, collecting an *e* card on the way if they need one.

Talk about rules, such as words ending in *ce* or *ge* needing to retain their final *e*, to keep the sounds soft, and others needing to lose them before an *i* or a *y* because two vowels should not go together. (Remind them that *y* often works in the same way as a vowel.) Then ask if anybody wants to change their mind about an *e* card for their word. Ask each pupil to say their new, longer word aloud and to ask everybody else if they think that its spelling is correct.

Extension/challenge
Write the word endings *tion* and *sion* onto cards and stick them onto separate walls. Make two lists of words such as: *imagination, station, creation, eviction, fiction, promotion, ration* and *television, mission, lesion, mansion, session, explosion, fusion*.

Call out the words one by one and ask the pupils to walk each time to whichever ending they think is correct for the word. Encourage them to move quickly and instinctively and not to hesitate and watch where others are going.

Score cards can be introduced to make the game more competitive. Give each child a score card and attach a sheet of spot or star stickers to the walls next to each ending. Each time the answer is given, the pupils standing in the correct place take one sticker each and put it onto their score card.

This game can also be played with other word endings, such as: *able/ible, ous/ious* or *ly/ily*.

Quietly does it

Learning objective
Silent letters as initials

Preparation
Make cards to represent words without their silent initial letters and others to represent the letters, such as *g*, *k* and *w*. Don't include proper nouns, to avoid the confusion of when to use capital letters, as that is not the focus of this activity.

Activity
Divide the pupils into two groups. Give a letter card to each pupil in the first group and a word card to each pupil in the second group. (If you are working with a whole class, the second group could be pairs of pupils or groups of three.)

Ask the pupils of the second group to mime their words without the initial letter, while the first group tiptoe or creep silently to join them. When the silent letter joins a word, the pupils should mime the new word together. For example:

night – pretend to sleep, then
knight – hold up an imaginary sword and shield

rap – pretend to knock on a door, then
wrap – cover an imaginary present and pretend to tie it with string

If the words are not real until the silent letter joins them, the second group should freeze until they can mime the words with the first group. For example: *nee/knee* or *naw/gnaw*.

Extension/challenge
Divide the pupils into three groups and invite each group to represent a different silent letter – *g*, *k* and *w*.

Make a list of words, such as: *gnat, know, write, gnaw, knot, wriggle, gnash, knee, wrap* and *knight*. Ensure that each letter is represented fairly equally and then write them out again in a random order.

Call out the words one by one and ask pupils to stand up each time they think the word begins with their silent letter, then to sit down again as a group. Or ask them to sit separately in spaces and to stand up at the right times without looking at others of their group.

Not a sound

Learning objective

Silent letters within words

Preparation

Talk with your pupils about silent letters that appear within or at the end of words, such as the *b* in *lamb* or *numb*, the *h* in *whisper*, the *l* in *salmon*, the *o* in *leopard* and the *gh* in *daughter*.

Prepare a list of words with silent letters, such as: *which, lightning, cupboard, rhyme, scissors* and *chemist*. Make several separate letter cards for each letter of the alphabet and lay the piles of letters out in spaces all over the floor.

Activity

Call out the words from your list one by one and invite pupils, by name, to tiptoe to fetch the correct silent letter or letters for them.

When a letter pile runs out, pupils may take letters from each other (asking politely – May I have the *p* please?)

Extension/challenge

Some pupils may still tend to write *f* or *ph* at the ends of *gh* words, or include an *r* instead of a *u*, because they only think phonetically. This activity aims to help them to be able to picture the words correctly.

Give a separate letter card to each pupil and ask them to form the words you call out by standing together in a line.

If you see 'larf' or 'coff' when you ask for *laugh* or *cough*, send the *u*, the *g* and the *h* over to the word to gently push away the *r* and the *f*. If you see 'tuph' when you ask for *tough*, send the *o* and the *g* over to gently push away the *p* and squeeze into their places in the line.

Teaching Grammar, Punctuation and Spelling Through Drama
© Debbie Chalmers and Brilliant Publications

Hide inside

Learning objective

Spelling longer words - by finding smaller words inside them

Preparation

Make cards that represent common beginnings of words, such as: *mis, un, str, th, pl* and *de*, and common endings, such as: *ing, ed* and *s*.

Also make words to fit with each of the beginnings. Some may fit more than one, such as:

> understand, read and take (mis)
> dress, conscious and curl (un)
> angle and anger (str)
> in, under and ought (th)
> ate, ease and ant (pl)
> lay, part and sign (de)

Check to make sure that they will also fit with at least one of the endings, but you will find that most words do.

Activity

Give one card to each pupil and discuss how some are real words, but the word beginnings and endings are not.

Ask the word beginnings to stand in a line at one side of the room and the endings at the other side. Then ask the words to walk through the middle and the beginnings and endings to call out when they see words that will fit and invite them to join them.

For example: groups of three pupils may create words like: *misunderstanding, uncurls, strangers, thundered, planting* and *delayed*. If one ending is used up first and the others will not fit with the words that are left (often *s*), encourage the pupils to discuss which swaps could be made to ensure that all of the words have one.

After the activity, talk with the pupils about breaking words into smaller parts to make their spellings easier. Offer extra clues to help them to remember the spellings of especially difficult words, such as: *There is **a rat** in sep**arat**e* and *Book two doubles for your ac**commo**dation.*

Extension/challenge

Offer pupils other word beginnings, such as: *dis, pre* or *spr*. Challenge each of them to think of a word beginning with one of these that they could act out for everybody to guess, both with and without the beginning, such as: *appointed* and *disappointed, sent* and *present* or *ray* and *spray*.

Repeat the activity with other endings, such as: *er, le* and *tre*.

Put us together

Learning objective

Spelling longer words – by joining words together

Preparation

Make a list of words that are formed by putting two shorter words together, such as: *football, handbag, seaside, snowman, carpet, cupboard* and *treehouse*. Read out the words to your pupils and invite them to contribute more ideas to add to the list.

Activity

Secretly say a different one of the shorter words to each pupil and ask them all to walk around miming their words and looking at everybody else's mimes. The aim of the game is to find a partner to make a longer word. When two pupils agree that they think they should become a pair, they may tell each other the words to check that they match.

When all of the pupils have formed pairs, invite them to take turns to mime both their shorter and longer words for the rest of the group to guess. For example: one pupil mimes *car*, then the other mimes *pet* and then they mime *carpet* together.

Extension/challenge

Divide the pupils into groups of three. Challenge each group to think of a three part word to act out together. They may act out two or three parts of the word separately first and then the whole word together. (Only some prefixes can be mimed and very few suffixes can.)

For example: *up* and *side* and *down* and then *upside down*, or *under* and *stand* and then *understanding*.

Teaching Grammar, Punctuation and Spelling Through Drama

What do you hear?

Learning objective
Homophones

Preparation
Explain and discuss homophones with your pupils and think up some together, such as: *rain/rein, here/hear, pair/pear* and *where/wear*. Write them onto a white board or a large sheet of paper attached to a wall as you say them aloud, so that pupils can see the differences between the spellings but hear that they sound the same.

Include some with only one spelling but more than one meaning, such as *train*, which can refer to a locomotive or mean to work at a sport.

Rub out the words or turn the paper around before beginning the game.

Activity
Invite the pupils to form pairs to choose and prepare a homophone together that they can act out for the rest of the group to watch. Ask one partner to act one word and then the other partner to act the other word.

Once somebody has guessed, ask each pupil to write their own word onto the white board or paper again, so that everybody can see and check the spellings. Ask the group to help each other if anybody is not sure.

Extension/challenge
Call out a word and invite pupils to act out as many of its meanings as they can. Some have two; others may have three or more. For example: mime *see* by looking around or using a telescope, mime *sea* by making wave movements, paddling or swimming and curl into the shape of a letter *c* on the floor.

Other words that work well include: *to/too/two* (moving towards a place, being together or the same and making the shape of the number or counting people or shoes, etc) and *pen* (for writing, an enclosure for animals and a female swan).

Which way round?

Learning objective
Words containing 'ie' or 'ei'

Preparation
Teach your pupils the rule *i before e except after c*, but remind them that it only works when the *ie* or *ei* sound rhymes with 'dee'.

Make lots of cards to represent words with the sound missing. For example:

> *bel - ve*
> *rel - f*
> *p – ce*
> *shr – k*

And also:

> *rec – ve*
> *rec – pt*
> *c – ling*

Jumble the cards and spread them out all over the floor.

Activity
Divide the pupils into two groups – the *ie* group and the *ei* group. The *ie* group could be a little larger, as there will probably be a greater number of those words. Ask the members of each group to work together to find all of their words. When all of the words have been collected, invite the pupils to sit down in their two groups and for each group to hold them up one by one for everybody to check. If any words are found to belong to the other group after all, they may be swapped.

Then invite each pupil to act out a different one of their group's words. They will need to discuss and negotiate to choose who takes which word. (If there are enough words, they may take more than one turn. If there are fewer words than pupils, invite them to work in pairs instead.)

Extension/challenge
Work with pupils to find and write down words that are exceptions to the rule, such as: *seize* and *pierce*, and words that do not follow the rule because the letters don't rhyme with 'dee', such as *beige, sleigh, neigh* and *eight*.

Encourage pupils to mime the words as they read them, in order to memorize them for use in their independent writing.

Catch the beats

Learning objective
Syllables

Preparation
Practise saying and clapping the syllables in names. Ask your pupils to decide how many syllables they have in the names that they are most usually known by and to form groups of those with one syllable, those with two, those with three and those with four or more. Encourage them to notice that each syllable always contains at least one vowel and that breaking words down in this way helps to make their spellings more obvious.

Invite each pupil to make a set of scorecards for himself, by writing the numerals 1–6 clearly onto separate circles or squares of card and attaching a drinking straw to the back of each one.

Encourage the pupils to help you to make a list of long words that can be broken down into three, four, five or six syllables, such as: *disappear, mountaineering, misunderstanding* and *encyclopedia*.

Activity
Read out words from your list, one at a time, and invite pupils to decide how many syllables and hold up the correct number card as quickly as they can. Say some shorter words, with only one or two syllables, randomly too. Include some similar words, such as: *training, straining, string, bring, pleasing* and *policing*, to encourage careful listening and concentration.

Increase the pace as pupils become more confident and encourage them to keep up for as long as possible, but just to laugh when they finally get into a muddle.

Extension/challenge
Divide the pupils into two equal teams and support both teams as they each prepare a list of words. Invite the teams to sit at opposite sides of the room, facing each other.

Ask the members of the first team to call out a word and the members of the second team to count the syllables and hold up their score cards. Then ask the second team to call out a word and the first team to score it.

Encourage pupils to work together within their teams and to take alternate turns quickly and confidently.

© Debbie Chalmers and Brilliant Publications

Index of learning objectives

Teaching Grammar, Punctuation and Spelling Through Drama
© Debbie Chalmers and Brilliant Publications

Lightning Source UK Ltd.
Milton Keynes UK
UKOW05f1414310116

267423UK00004B/36/P

9 781783 170227